This book! Val has written a classic—the book we all need most. There is no more important relationship than with our Father, yet it's one of the most mysterious. Val has broken down the walls of fear, hesitation, and insecurity we so often face with prayer. Get ready to experience freedom as Val skillfully guides you to God's truth about our most important conversation. With practical, real-world wisdom, *Pray Confidently and Consistently* will equip you to deepen your faith or cultivate it for the first time! A must-read!

LARA CASEY, author of *Cultivate and Make It Happen*

Powerful, biblical, and practical, *Pray Confidently and Consistently* will ignite a desire in your heart to be a prayer warrior in daily life. In this book, Val exposes the weights that burden us and keep us from praying with confidence, and she leads us into freedom as we talk to God. I've been waiting for a book like this to recommend to many women and know this will lead us into a deeper walk with God!

GRETCHEN SAFFLES, author of *The Well-Watered Woman*, founder of Well-Watered Women

Seeking to deepen her own prayer life, the great writer Flannery O'Connor once penned in her journal, "Can't anyone teach me how to pray?" No doubt, Flannery needed this book. In a refreshing guide to prayer that will embolden you to seek more conversation with God, Valerie takes us into the raw and personal parts of her journey. She is both a guide and friend as she uncovers and dives deep into the hard-to-talk-about topics. Her words are both inspiring and encouraging, and this book is one you will pull off the shelf again and again. The wisdom within these pages is the kindling for the fire you need to take your prayer life to the next level.

HANNAH BRENCHER, author of *Fighting Forward* and *Come Matter Here*

What's causing you to neglect prayer? Pause to think about your answer, and then dig into this book to find in Val Woerner a trusty companion who will walk you through the process of overcoming that obstacle to nurture a thriving prayer life.

ASHERITAH CIUCIU, author and host of the Prayers of *REST* podcast

I am delighted to see a resource on prayer that is approachable, practical, and dedicated to the truth of God's Word. This would be an excellent starting point for both new believers and long-time Christians who desire to know God intimately through prayer. Val doesn't just teach it—she lives it, and it comes through in her book.

PHYLICIA MASONHEIMER, author and founder of Every Woman a Theologian

We too easily stand at a distance from the most important topic of the hour: How can we talk to our God? And Val shows us how to close that distance—not as a dispassionate expert but, instead, as a real human who is desperate to talk to God, just like you and me. This book is a needed guide for days like the ones in which we've found ourselves.

SARA HAGERTY, bestselling author of *Unseen*

Inside these pages, Val shares God's truth that shaped her own prayer life. While guiding you to realize the same consistency and confidence is possible for you, she's honest enough to let you know of the struggles you'll inevitably encounter. Get ready to be encouraged and challenged by this real conversation about prayer to better know the even more real God who is listening.

MICHELLE MYERS, founder of She works HIS way

I believe that talking to God should be simple. It should feel accessible. It should come naturally to us! And yet we live in a fallen world where we've forgotten that he is as near to us as our own bodies and breath. So we need guides . . . encouragers . . . women with wisdom to remind us of the power and practicality of prayer. Val has been that guide for me the last few years—first through her products and now through this book. I am so grateful for her and cannot suggest reading her words enough!

JESS CONNOLLY, author of *You Are the Girl for the Job* and *Breaking Free from Body Shame*

pray confidently & consistently

Tyndale | MOMENTUM

A Tyndale nonfiction imprint

valerie woerner

pray confidently & consistently

finally let go of the things

holding you back from your

most important conversation

Visit Tyndale online at tyndale.com.

Visit Tyndale Momentum online at tyndalemomentum.com.

TYNDALE, Tyndale's quill logo, *Tyndale Momentum*, and the Tyndale Momentum logo are registered trademarks of Tyndale House Ministries. Tyndale Momentum is the nonfiction imprint of Tyndale House Publishers, Carol Stream, Illinois.

Designed by Julie Chen

Published in association with Folio Literary Management, LLC, 630 9th Avenue, Suite 1101, New York, NY 10036.

For information about special discounts for bulk purchases, please contact Tyndale House Publishers at csresponse@tyndale.com, or call 1-855-277-9400.

Library of Congress Cataloging-in-Publication Data

A catalog record for this book is available from the Library of Congress.

ISBN 978-1-4964-5199-6

Printed in the United States of America

27	26	25	24	23	22	21
7	6	5	4	3	2	1

To my mom, who instilled in me the belief

that God heard and responded to my prayers.

———————————————

Therefore, since we are surrounded by such a huge crowd of witnesses to the life of faith, let us strip off every weight that slows us down, especially the sin that so easily trips us up. And let us run with endurance the race God has set before us. We do this by keeping our eyes on Jesus, the champion who initiates and perfects our faith. Because of the joy awaiting him, he endured the cross, disregarding its shame. Now he is seated in the place of honor beside God's throne.

HEBREWS 12:1-2, NLT

contents

ENGAGE

PERSIST

Introduction

I DON'T RUN. Don't get me wrong. I *have* run before but don't make it a habit.

It wasn't always this way. I have a fond memory of running barefoot through the seemingly never-ending hall of the middle school building our church met in when I was eight. It felt as if just the tips of my toes hit the linoleum floor with each step, as if it took everything in me to slow down enough so that I didn't actually lift off the ground. I felt weightless, unstoppable, and even superhuman.

I'd give anything to run that way again. Twenty-seven years later, I feel beyond clunky. I feel the weight of pounding the pavement in my flimsy knees. I feel my flesh rise and fall, and I even get dizzy when I hit the ground. I feel the air, all right, but it's heavy and thick like humidity, and it seems to push me down.

Have you ever felt that way before—not on the pavement but in your prayer life? Have you felt the weight of distractions and responsibilities thick like a humid southern Louisiana morning? Something you just can't seem to cut through?

I sure have.

I desperately want to feel weightless and unhindered in my prayer life, but instead, these things I can't even see keep dragging me down.

I neglect to pray because I need to spend time on a screen keeping tabs on people I hardly know.

I hit snooze, assuming those last few restless minutes in bed will refresh me more than time with God.

I offer trite prayers because I know I *should* say something, but I forget that prayer actually has power.

Prayer can be one of the hardest spiritual disciplines in the Christian life. If you have felt that way, you are absolutely not alone.

It makes sense. I can measure so many things, even in my walk with God, but not prayer. I know when I've read a few chapters of the Bible. I know how much I tithe. And you'd better believe I know if I skipped a meal and fasted instead. But the gates of prayer are wide open. The structure can be so fluid that I sometimes don't know if I can even label what just happened as prayer time because somewhere in the last five minutes, I drifted off to my to-do list.

If you're nodding along thinking, *This gal read my diary*, I promise I didn't. But I have read my own. I've struggled to take my own prayer life seriously. I've struggled to understand its power. And sometimes I recognize its power and *still* choose my dumb cell phone.

Since I created a prayer journal seven years ago, my own prayer life has grown. And my simple desire to share a product that helped me focus in prayer morphed into a mission to understand the everyday struggles women face so I could cheer them along in this conversation of a lifetime. Since then, I've put together multiple prayer-oriented products, developed a prayer course, and created an online community where women can support each other through the challenges they face in prayer. After years of facilitating these conversations, one thing I know for sure is that there are external *and* internal distractions causing

> We don't have to limp through our prayer lives carrying unnecessary weights.

us to miss out on a prayer life that goes beyond anything we can fathom—and this book will focus on the internal things our prayer journals weren't able to address.

In 2019, Crossway surveyed fourteen thousand people about their prayer lives, and 2 percent were "very satisfied."[1] Two percent. That means you likely fall in the camp with those of us who are not satisfied and are longing for more.

Another stat revealed that 30 percent of people surveyed said they hadn't even spent ten continuous minutes in prayer in the last week.[2] I won't dare ask how many continuous minutes we've spent on our phones this week. Yikes, right?

That's the bad news.

But here's the good news. We don't have to limp through our prayer lives carrying unnecesary weigths—such as unfounded expectations, our desire for control, distractions, or pride. When we throw these weights aside, we can move forward at a steady pace.

Hebrews 12:1-2, which I'm using as the key passage for the book, gives the sweetest visual of running unencumbered:

Therefore, since we are surrounded by such a huge
crowd of witnesses to the life of faith, let us strip
off every weight that slows us down, especially the
sin that so easily trips us up. And let us run with
endurance the race God has set before us. We do
this by keeping our eyes on Jesus, the champion who
initiates and perfects our faith. Because of the joy
awaiting him, he endured the cross, disregarding its
shame. Now he is seated in the place of honor beside
God's throne.

NLT

Back in ancient times, when the book of Hebrews was written, many men wore long outfits with fabric that hung down. I
imagine basically muumuus. When athletes raced, they would
throw off as many clothes as possible so they could run without
hindrance.[3] Word on the street is that some ancient Greeks,
surely the most competitive, even ran nude.[*]

A moment from *The Biggest Loser* helps me further visualize this. Near the end of one competition, the contestants,
who by now were significantly lighter than when they started,
ran carrying weights that equaled the number of pounds
they'd lost during their time on the show. With each mile,
they removed some of the weight until, finally, they threw it
all off and could run free.[4] It was emotional to see what could
happen when the competitors weren't so burdened. And it
wasn't just the physical weight; you could see they'd also been
freed from emotional weights.

I want us to run free too.

I want our prayer lives to be unencumbered by the

---

[*]Or nekkid, if you're from the South like me.

distractions that threaten to steal precious time with the Lord in favor of trivial things. I want us to learn to pray with confidence and really know the God we're praying to. I want our prayer lives to be rich and deep and to transform the way we think. I want us to love God so much that we can't imagine not being in conversation with him every day. I want us to experience the joy of persistent, consistent prayer that glorifies God.

Throwing Off the Weights

Did you ever wonder why prayer is so hard? After all, it's just talking and listening to God. Why is it so much easier to reach for my to-do list, remote, phone, or even a really good book? The short answer is that our enemy knows prayer is powerful. He knows what will happen if we pray, and he's scared. He's attempting to sabotage our races because he knows that once the weights come off, he doesn't have a prayer.

In *The Compound Effect*, Darren Hardy writes about how this idea of compounding helps us when we're trying to develop any habit:

> It's like the wheels of a steam locomotive. At a standstill, it takes very little to keep it from moving forward—a one-inch block of wood placed under the front wheel will do the job. . . . But once the train starts rolling, the wheels get into a rhythm. If the pressure remains consistent, the train gains momentum, and watch out! At 55 miles an hour, that train can crash through a five-foot, steel-reinforced concrete wall and keep on going.[5]

We can be stopped by a little piece of wood, or we can plow through steel and concrete. We can get distracted by a fly buzzing around our bedroom or by dishes in the sink, or we can pray with *Tangled* playing in the background, while we're facing a full inbox, or even through big moments of fear.

I want to plow through my distractions. I need to.

Our intimacy with God is dependent on our prayer lives. We cannot have a close relationship with him—we cannot experience his power, his wisdom, his peace, his joy—if we aren't *going* to him.

Prayer invites action into our lives by the God who is more powerful than we could ever be on our own.

Prayer invites action into our lives by the God who is more powerful than we could ever be on our own. I don't want us to miss out on those possibilities! What are the weights we need to throw off so they don't hold us back from a deeper conversation with God? What distractions are slowing us down like a thick humidity when we could be running freely with our Father?

Stephen Nielsen says the weight referenced in Hebrews 12:1 "is an impediment, or a hindrance, or an encumbrance . . . that which keeps us from hearing the voice of God or that keeps us from desiring to hear His voice. It is whatever dulls our spiritual senses, puts us on the path of sin, saps our endurance, and keeps us from looking toward Jesus."[6]

Friend, what weight, if identified, would lose its power and become merely something that threatened to take you out but fell completely flat? The weight of expectations, distractions, or emotions? What about the weight of facades or valleys? In the chapters ahead, we're going to talk about fifteen specific weights on our prayer lives, what they cause us to miss out on, and how we can remove them.

We all know that prayer is more important than Netflix or sleeping in. I think we'd get that Sunday school question right every time. But in this book, I hope you'll find the motivation to actually figure out how to make it a priority in your everyday life. (A quick note as we go forward: Have your Bible handy! I learned so much about prayer as I studied Scripture this year, so you're going to get a ton of it. Dive into the full passages if you can. One of the biggest ways we transform our prayer lives is by knowing God's Word.)

Now let's take off the weights that are suffocating our prayer lives and leaving us gasping for Jesus. It's not worth walking through this life in our own feeble strength when the God of the universe is beckoning us to come sit with him, share our needs and our hearts, and simply know him.

Why pray?

- Because God said so (1 Thessalonians 5:16-18). If this were the only reason we had, it would be enough.
- Because it brings glory to God (John 14:13).
- Because we were created for communion with God (Revelation 21:3-4).
- Because prayer changes things (James 5:16).
- Because it's the way we live at the center of God's will (Proverbs 3:5-6).
- Because we are needy, and only God can help us (Matthew 11:28-30).

———————

We see spiritual giants of the past who seemed to live with peace, purpose, and effectiveness because of their close communion with God. We want that kind of life, but it doesn't happen through fractured prayers or drive-by conversations. It requires waiting and fervency and time. We don't like to say that for fear of overwhelming those who already feel overwhelmed by life, kids, and a job. But the truth is, if I don't mention it, you're left thinking that part-time prayer isn't all it's cracked up to be, or worse, that God lied when he told us throughout Scripture that he wants us to ask. The worthwhile things in life require effort.

I want to run with the Lord like my eight-year-old self, who felt as though nothing could hold her back. And I'm finally embracing the intentionality it will take to do it. I'm grateful that those weights that so easily entangle me can actually be removed. How hope-filled is that?

We might be weighed down right now, but that isn't the end of the story.

The weights are coming off.

And we're about to run like our feet barely touch the linoleum.

Father, thank you for each person reading these words right now. I pray you would fill them with hope for the possibility of going deeper with you. Give them a passion that helps them soar, and, Father, protect them from our very present enemy who's desperately doing all he can along our way so that we slow down, stop, or turn around all together. Draw us nearer to you. In Jesus' name, let's do this!

approach

**throwing off the weights that keep us
from coming to God with confidence**

1

Where's My Genie in a Bottle?

Understanding Who I'm Praying To

I WASN'T QUITE OLD ENOUGH to drive yet, but I had one thing on my mind: a hunter-green Saturn. It was my dream car, and I wanted one so bad that I could smell the gasoline and toxin-laden air fresheners.

How did I land on a Saturn? After surveying the showroom that was the car pickup line at school, I set my sights on the Saturn my friend Tiffany's mom drove. It felt so put-together with its sleek hood and tidy doors. I'd checked out the menu and had my order ready to beam up to the Big Guy in the sky: one hunter-green Saturn, please. No substitutions.

At thirteen, I thought I had a deep understanding of prayer and a faith that could move mountains—or at the very least, a faith that I hoped would move a Saturn into my family's driveway. I must have recently heard John 15:7, "Ask whatever you wish, and it will be done for you." I glossed over that whole "If you abide in me, and my words abide in you" part in the first part of the verse, but how important could that be? God was telling me to *ask for anything*! The way I interpreted it was, if you have enough faith, *your prayer will come true*. That should have been my first clue how off I was. "Will come true"? I'm pretty sure I only remember that line from magic-filled fairy tales.

Regardless, I was ready for my green Saturn. And let me ease all your minds as you think, *Uh . . . you were only thirteen.* Relax. I had an airtight plan. My dad had a machine shop with the perfect air-conditioned spot to store my new Saturn till I could actually drive it. Everything was falling into place. *The stars were aligning.* Maybe that should have been my second clue as to how I viewed God. I had a plan, and now, if God would just do what I'd read he could do, we'd be great.

That was when it happened. I remember being in the upstairs bedroom I shared with my twin sister. Our white wicker daybeds faced each other, and right at the top of the walls was the most mature trellis border of maroon, navy, and hunter green you had ever seen grace a thirteen-year-old's walls. I sat on my bed and prayed. And I believed with all my heart that God *could* give me the hunter-green Saturn of my dreams. I really believed he was powerful enough to do it. So when I said, "Amen," I ran downstairs with the gusto of the disciples running to the empty tomb and opened the door to go test-drive (or sit in) my new Saturn.

And would you believe it? It wasn't there!

At this point, I had some ideas to wrestle with. Why, despite my big, faith-filled prayers, did God not give me my

Saturn? And how was I supposed to keep praying when it looked like the genie had run out of magic?

This is the weight of expectations.

We miss out on fostering our most important relationship when we start with inaccurate assumptions.

This experience could have shaken me or even turned me off to prayer completely. I mean, *God didn't even answer me like he promised he would!* But I had a praying momma, and I think the way she kept going to God helped me keep going to him too. Regardless of the fact that *he totally ignored me even when I believed him most.*

Notice it? Go back and read the italicized phrases. Did anything make you wince as you read my story? Or did it go undetected because these are weights you carry too?

I had expectations of God that were in no way based on reality. They were things I made up or assumed from an isolated verse in Scripture. I convinced myself that if God didn't answer my specific request, he either didn't care or didn't hear. Neither was a great quality for the God of the universe, in my humble opinion.

At the ripe old age of thirteen, I still had a lot to learn about God. I'm thirty-six, and that's still true! But in those early years, I prayed to a one-dimensional God who I thought was there to give me anything I asked for.

> What we subconsciously believe to be true about God determines whether we will view prayer as essential and fulfilling or worthless and dull.

What we subconsciously believe to be true about God determines whether we will view prayer as essential and fulfilling or worthless and dull. When we have accurate expectations of who we're praying to (as much as is humanly possible), we will pray differently. When I don't understand who I'm praying to, I ask for a hunter-green Saturn and then assume that if I don't get it, God's ears were clogged, he fell asleep during the conversation, or he didn't really mean what he said in the first place when he told me to ask.

I miss out on who God really is when I bury him in my own unrealistic expectations.

So who is he really? And what makes him worthy of my prayers in the first place? Let's talk about six prime characteristics of God that will affect how we pray.

1. God Is the Creator and Savior

We're getting back to basics, which may feel like overkill, but it will lay a solid foundation for our prayers. Genesis 1:27 (yep, all the way back) says, "So God created man in his own image, in the image of God he created him; male and female he created them." We weren't accidentally created by some unknown force. We were intentionally formed and created for relationship with God.

Sin messed up that relationship, and the reality is that we've all sinned (see Romans 3:23). Because sin leads to death and separation from him (see Romans 6:23), God sent his Son to pay the price for our sins (see Romans 5:8) so that if we confess our faith in him (Romans 10:9-10), we will be saved (see Romans 10:13). Friend, without salvation in Jesus Christ alone, we can't experience a restored relationship with God. That means salvation is essential to an actual prayer relationship with God.*

So not only did God create us, but he also sent his Son to

---

*We just mall-walked through a quick telling of the gospel, known as the Romans Road. If you're not a Christian and want to know more, ask a friend or pastor to share with you. It is the most important decision you will ever make.

die so that the relationship our sin broke could be restored. Can we take a second to reflect on that? We'll talk more about God's love for us later, but if this doesn't reveal the heart of God for us, I don't know what does. I want a relationship with this guy. I'm honestly amazed it's even available to me, and I never again want to see him as just a genie who grants wishes.

2. God Hears Us

The God of the universe, creator of all things, longs to sit in the quiet moments with you and me. And because he's God, he can do that for every single one of his kids. We'll never get a busy signal or an "out to lunch" sign. He is always ready to spend time with us when we choose to.

God hears

Take a gander at several biblical examples of God hearing people's prayers and responding. His kindness is overwhelming, no? We get to pray to the same God—the one who hears.

Isaac prayed to the LORD for his wife, because she was barren. And the LORD granted his prayer, and Rebekah his wife conceived.
GENESIS 25:21

Moses went out from Pharaoh and prayed to the LORD. And the LORD did as Moses asked, and removed the swarms of flies from Pharaoh, from his servants, and from his people; not one remained.
EXODUS 8:30-31

As the sound of the trumpet grew louder and louder, Moses spoke, and God answered him in thunder.
EXODUS 19:19

David built there an altar to the LORD and presented burnt offerings and peace offerings and called on the LORD, and the LORD answered him with fire from heaven upon the altar of burnt offering.

1 CHRONICLES 21:26

So Samuel took a nursing lamb and offered it as a whole burnt offering to the LORD. And Samuel cried out to the LORD for Israel, and the LORD answered him.

1 SAMUEL 7:9

[David said,] In my distress I called upon the LORD; to my God I called. From his temple he heard my voice, and my cry came to his ears. . . . He brought me out into a broad place; he rescued me, because he delighted in me.

2 SAMUEL 22:7, 20

[The Lord says,] "Then you will call upon me and come and pray to me, and I will hear you. You will seek me and find me, when you seek me with all your heart."

JEREMIAH 29:12-13

Then Jonah prayed to the LORD his God from the belly of the fish, saying, "I called out to the LORD, out of my distress, and he answered me; out of the belly of Sheol I cried, and you heard my voice."

JONAH 2:1-2

Psalm 34:15 says, "The eyes of the LORD are toward the righteous and his ears toward their cry." (Good news, friend: *Righteous* does not mean perfect but, rather, those who are seeking God.) As you search Scripture, make a note each time you see wording such as "God hears" or "God listened" or a reference to God's "ears." Noticing these as I study the Bible has shown me just how much God is inviting us into conversation.

This is both heartwarming and heartbreaking because I

know my devotion to God isn't nearly as . . . well, devoted as his is to me. If you're reading this book, I bet you feel the same. Hold tight. Our next point brings lots of freedom.

3. God Loves Us Unconditionally

We get to pray to a God to whom we cannot say anything so audacious that he'll take his ball and go home. I have two little girls—Vivi, seven, and Vana, four—and at bedtime when I say goodnight, I tell them, "You'll never lose my love." We've gotten silly with it and started to say, "You'll never lose my lllll . . . unch" or "my . . . socks" just to be funny, but it never fails to put them at ease to know they can never mess up so badly that I won't love them. One day, they will mess up royally, and I don't want them to be tempted to try to handle it on their own because they're afraid it will change my love. Instead, my hope is that they will have grown up knowing no mistake will drive me away and that they will always remember it's safe to return to me.

Even more than we need to know a parent's love is unconditional, we need to know that God's love is. Have you ever felt that you can't go to God until you clean yourself up, or that it's been such a long time since you prayed that you'd feel embarrassed coming to him now? Or maybe you feel like you hate to come to him only when you're in a crisis, so you try to face the hard stuff alone.

If that's you right now, stop here. Don't read another sentence before you close your eyes and ask God to draw you near. Your Father's love was never built on your performance in the first place. What great news! Dive into Scripture and get to know how deep and wide the Father's love is for us. Ephesians 3:14-19 is a great place to start.

4. God Is All-Knowing

I like to think I'm pretty discerning and can come up with some top-notch plans. I make assumptions about what needs to happen in my life and then bring requests based on a thought-out blueprint that I'm sure will impress the pants off God. (That was highly inappropriate, but it reveals just how cavalier I can be sometimes with God.)

This controlling nature leads me to get upset when the answer to my prayers is no. *Surely* if God had all the facts, he'd see things differently. I'd never say this out loud, of course, but subconsciously, I must assume it if I question an all-knowing God's plans, right?

The reality is that not a moment of our lives is hidden from God. He's witness to it all.

You hem me in, behind and before,
    and lay your hand upon me.
Such knowledge is too wonderful for me;
    it is high; I cannot attain it.

Where shall I go from your Spirit?
    Or where shall I flee from your presence?
If I ascend to heaven, you are there!
    If I make my bed in Sheol, you are there!
If I take the wings of the morning
    and dwell in the uttermost parts of the sea,
even there your hand shall lead me,
    and your right hand shall hold me.
If I say, "Surely the darkness shall cover me,

and the light about me be night,"
even the darkness is not dark to you;
    the night is bright as the day,
    for darkness is as light with you.

For you formed my inward parts;
    you knitted me together in my mother's womb.
I praise you, for I am fearfully and wonderfully made.
Wonderful are your works;
    my soul knows it very well.
My frame was not hidden from you,
when I was being made in secret,
    intricately woven in the depths of the earth.
Your eyes saw my unformed substance;
in your book were written, every one of them,
    the days that were formed for me,
    when as yet there was none of them.
PSALM 139:5-16

That passage is long, but soak it in. We are known by God. We're living in a time when people are desperate to be known and longing to be seen. It's why social media apps have "like" buttons and hearts. And it's why we incessantly check to see how people are responding to what we share. Are people seeing me? How many people are seeing me? What do they think when they see me? That desire is part of our human nature. Unfortunately, we look for it in all the wrong places and accept a shallow version of being known because we forget that we are already so intimately known by our almighty God.

5. God Is Capable

When we pray, we aren't just talking to a nice guy who cares about us and knows us well. We're praying to an almighty God who has the power to drop hailstones from heaven. You weren't expecting *that* for my example, were you? In the book of Joshua, the Israelites were starting to move into the land God had promised them, and some of the Canaanite nations banded together to attack them. The Israelites defeated them, and Joshua 10:11 says, "As [the enemy armies] fled before Israel, while they were going down the ascent of Beth-horon, the LORD threw down large stones from heaven on them as far as Azekah, and they died. There were more who died because of the hailstones than the sons of Israel killed with the sword."

You aren't praying to a statue or a lifeless, mythical God. You're praying to a God who acts throughout Scripture on his people's behalf.

The passage goes on:

> At that time Joshua spoke to the LORD in the day when the LORD gave the Amorites over to the sons of Israel, and he said in the sight of Israel,

> "Sun, stand still at Gibeon,
>   and moon, in the Valley of Aijalon."
> And the sun stood still, and the moon stopped,
>   until the nation took vengeance on their enemies.

> Is this not written in the Book of Jashar? The sun stopped in the midst of heaven and did not hurry to

set for about a whole day. There has been no day like it before or since, *when the* LORD *heeded the voice of a man, for the* LORD *fought for Israel.*
JOSHUA 10:12-14, EMPHASIS ADDED

God follows up the first miracle by having the sun stand still until the battle is over. Can you even imagine? How many visuals do we need to convince us that God is capable of coming to our aid? But here's the kicker: This was a response to prayer. The Lord heeded Joshua and fought for Israel.

You aren't praying to a statue or a lifeless, mythical God. You're praying to a God who acts throughout Scripture on his people's behalf. In those moments when you can't help but feel you're praying to the ceiling or talking to yourself, draw close to this image of a God who fought for Israel. I know he's fighting for us, too.

6. God Is Unchangeable

The God who healed your momma's best friend, Monica; Mary and Martha's brother, Lazarus; and Moses' sister, Miriam, is the same God you lift your requests to. This is just one more reason it's important to study the Word—so we know the stories of God's work in the past and remember that God is still with us.

He's never changing. He is the solid rock on which we stand. As I write this book during the COVID-19 shelter-at-home orders, I cannot tell you how many times I've broken into the old hymn

On Christ, the solid Rock, I stand;
all other ground is sinking sand,
all other ground is sinking sand.[1]

Let's pause

There will be many moments throughout this book when I'll invite us to pause, and they aren't for dramatic effect. I know the place we will truly learn to pray is in prayer, and so I want us to wrestle with these truths in God's presence.

One day I was looking through a set of flashcards I'd bought to teach my girls Greek and Hebrew. (That probably sounds more impressive than it is. The Tiny Theologians company makes this easy to do!) One card said that "Selah," which is a Hebrew word referenced in the Psalms, is a command meaning *to pause and reflect or pause and consider.*[2] It is used at important places in the Psalms where readers should stop and think about what they are reading. When I read the Psalms after learning this, I started noticing "Selah" every-where. (Depending on your Bible translation, you might also see the word "Interlude.") I imagined what David and the other psalmists were thinking as they jotted down that word and the thoughts that followed.

Psalm 32:7 says, "You are a hiding place for me; you pre-serve me from trouble; you surround me with shouts of deliv-erance. *Selah.*" Did David need a moment to really let that sink in? In this psalm of forgiveness, maybe he spoke words he knew were true but still needed to let his heart catch up to what his mind knew.

So as you're reading these chapters, if you see "Selah," that's your cue to pause, reflect, and even pray about what's being shared.

When so much has shifted, bringing changes I never knew were even possible (like ending a school year two months early and becoming a teacher overnight), I am finding my foothold on the unchangeable Rock.

People, even faithful believers, will fail us. And maybe we give God a bad rap because we've experienced hard things in community with his kids, but God is our solid Rock. We can trust him. And that alters not only our prayers but also our response to the results of our prayers. "No" answers don't have to make us doubt his existence. We don't have to question whether the God who redeemed us has suddenly decided to put some conditions on his great love. He hasn't. He's the same.

And, friend, this is who we get to pray to.

He invites us to commune with him on a constant, daily basis. He encourages us to pray at all times and without ceasing (see 1 Thessalonians 5:17-18).

Can we just take another minute to relish that and thank him profusely for it?

Selah.

What a mighty God we get to pray to.

Back when I was thirteen and treated him like a genie, he was compassionate to listen to my prayer, no matter how ridiculous, and was unconditional in his love. He knew vastly more than I did. He is still the same God I read about in the Bible, and the fact that he is capable of causing the sun to stand still yet *still* didn't give me that car lets me know it wasn't that he couldn't do it. It just wasn't part of his plan. I now understand better why.

Remembering these truths about God will radically shift our prayers. There will be no room for pride and accusations when we don't get the result we want. No reason to hold back. No fear of uncertainty. And no wimpy prayers.

Even the demons believe in God (see James 2:19). But us? We don't just believe in him. We know who he is. We trust that he is worthy of our prayers and know that we're pretty blessed to even have the opportunity to talk to him!

The genie whose lamp I rubbed, believing I'd get a Saturn, turns out to not be a genie at all. He's an all-knowing, all-loving, fully capable, unchanging God. When we throw off the weight of our inaccurate assumptions about God, we'll know without a doubt that he's worthy of all our prayers.

reflect

Which quality of God has gone unnoticed in your life? How has that affected your prayers?

When have you prayed for something and gotten a "no"?

How do the following characteristics of God help remove the weight of expectations?

- *God is the Creator and Savior*
- *God hears us*
- *God loves us unconditionally*
- *God is all-knowing*
- *God is capable*
- *God is unchangeable*

read

○ Psalm 147:5
○ Zephaniah 3:17
○ Romans 5:8

○ Romans 8:1-17
○ 1 John 3:20

2

Am I Doing This Right?

Discovering a Right Posture for Prayer

BACK WHEN I KNEW EVERYTHING, around the age of eighteen, my prayer formula was basic but neatly written out in chalk each morning in homeroom. In my Christian high school, the day began with a call for prayer requests. The teacher would ask for a volunteer to pray, and I was the annoying girl who loved to do it because it came with perks like writing on the chalkboard, which still held some magic even in high school. I'd write the requests on the board as they came in and then pray out loud for all of them. I had a formula: Offer a quick thank you, use the term "Father God" as needed throughout the prayer, and hit all the requests with appropriate tone. Sick Aunt Mabel gets slightly more somberness and time than the Johnsons heading on vacation and for sure more than pets. I knew the pattern and was confident it qualified me to pray.

I think that's why my hand shot up to pray more often

than most of my classmates'. I thought I had it down perfectly. What I didn't realize, though, was that my motives were reminiscent of the Pharisees. Thinking I was perfect sabotaged my prayers. I had no room to learn anything and absolutely zero amount of the much-needed ingredient for prayer, humility. On the other side of the coin, though, is the paralysis some people feel when they think they're supposed to come to God in just the right way.

This is the weight of perfectionism.

We miss out on a right heart posture when we think we can—and should—come to God perfectly.

The weight of perfectionism convinces us that we need to find the right words before we come to God in prayer.

The weight of perfectionism tells us it's better to stay quiet till we figure things out on our own.

The weight of perfectionism silences us because we assume we *can* clean ourselves enough to approach God.

What should I say when I pray? What if I say the wrong thing or use the wrong format? Why even try if there's a good chance I'll mess it all up anyway and actually make things worse? And how do I move past the paralyzing feeling that I don't know what I'm doing?

We can talk a lot about the outer distractions that keep us from praying, but our internal dialogue can be paralyzing to our prayers too. Over the past few years, as I've been studying prayer, I've had countless conversations with friends, family members, and blog readers about what holds them back most when they pray. One of the most common responses is never knowing what to say and being afraid of messing up.

What gave us this idea that we need to attain perfection in our prayers in the first place? What made us think that the

God of the universe is expecting us to hold our own in this conversation and to have a greeting card–worthy response?

Here's my theory: We read Jesus' instructions on prayer in the New Testament, especially in the Sermon on the Mount, and see some pretty serious "do nots." But we forget to read these in the context of the entire Bible. Okay, "read something in light of all of Scripture" is a pretty tall order, but I think when we step back and read all of Jesus' instructions together, we get the full intended picture. It's not the methods that God prescribes as much as the heart behind them.

- When Jesus tells us to pray privately rather than publicly (see Matthew 6:5-6), he's not telling us to avoid praying corporately. He's saying to avoid performance-driven prayers.

- When Jesus tells us to avoid vain repetition (see Matthew 6:7), he's not warning us against praying again and again about the same concerns. He's telling us not to think we can make God hear us by praying repetitively.

- When Jesus tells us not to go public with our fasting (see Matthew 6:16-18), he's not saying we can't talk about the impact fasting has on our lives. He's saying we shouldn't fast to look good to the crowds.

This seemingly specific formula for prayer that we see Jesus share in the Gospels—both in the Sermon on the Mount and in his model prayer for his disciples, which we call the Lord's Prayer—should encourage us the way we felt encouraged as children when a parent taught us how to ride a bike or crack an egg. Mom or Dad laid out careful instructions designed to help us do something we previously didn't know how to do *and* then walked us through it. How special is that? My guess is, as a parent, if your kids come ready to learn the art of egg-cracking and their attempt results in spilling a little shell in the batter, you don't fly off the handle. You're teaching them how to do something new, not waiting to see them fail.

God isn't waiting for us to fail either. He created us. He could have told us to figure prayer out for ourselves if he didn't care about us, but he's rooting for us. Part of removing the weight of perfectionism is tuning in more to who God is than who we are. It's so simple. It's not about following a bunch of rules but about looking at someone besides ourselves: God.

If you feel paralyzed in prayer, stop asking, "How am I doing?" and start asking, "God, who are you?" The more we know about him, the more I think we can approach him like children who audaciously run to their father because they aren't worried about impressing him with their perfection. They know full well that that's a completely silly thing to do with this father who loves them unconditionally.

> If you feel paralyzed in prayer, stop asking, "How am I doing?" and start asking, "God, who are you?"

I believe the "right" or "perfect" way to pray is far less logistical than we'd assume and has more to do with our heart posture than our specific words or methods. I think a few things are key: We come humbly, we confess often, and we have faith. If we can do these three things, we can pray without paralysis.

1. Come Humbly

Last year, I read a tiny book on humility by Andrew Murray. If I can be perfectly honest, I never would have picked up a two-hundred-page book on humility because the topic didn't seem as important as some others. This book was pamphlet-sized and was staring me in the face at my parents' house one Sunday.

Thankfully, the road to picking up that book was easy. As I started reading, it didn't take me long to be convinced that humility is the basis of our faith and life.

Trusty old Wikipedia says, "Dictionary definitions accentuate humility as a low self-regard and sense of unworthiness. In a religious context humility can mean a recognition of self in relation to a deity (i.e. God) or deities, and subsequent submission to said deity as a member of that religion."[1] I could not love this any more. The world sees humility as a sense of unworthiness, while in a "religious" context, it means seeing ourselves in relation to God and submitting.

That's pretty profound, Wiki. At the same time, it's so simple. Humility means having an accurate picture of reality. The reality is that God is all-powerful and I am limited. I choose to admit that fact and make the obvious choice to follow the one who reigns supreme.

Imagine what it means to come to prayer with humility. To approach the throne of God without worrying if your doubts

---

tip —————————————————————

If you find it hard to get into a mindset of humility, read and pray through some verses that highlight God's majesty compared to our smallness. Psalm 8 is a great option!

---

are disrespectful because you know you have a genuine desire to pursue the Lord. To be less concerned with yourself in prayer and completely consumed with the God in front of you. To stop trying to win God over with perfect words because you fully understand you couldn't possibly earn his grace.

Humility is a cure-all. Start a prayer with it, and watch what happens.

I'm convinced that humility is essential to praying without fear of messing it all up. Humility is the first step we take that ensures whatever comes next is pleasing to the Lord. I may not know exactly what to say, but if I can come humbly, I don't have to agonize about it. I don't need to micromanage making sure I'm coming with pure motives (see James 4:3). I don't need to make sure I'm not just praying for show (see Matthew 6:5). Since these are the antithesis of humility, we start by coming humbly and then we don't worry about over-analyzing the rest.

In George Mueller's book *Answers to Prayer*, he says, "I seek at the beginning to get my heart into such a state that it has no will of its own in regard to a given matter."[2] Yowza. That is solid. Can you imagine praying consistently like that? Without telling God what we think he should do, but trusting that he is in charge and will do what is right? I long for this type of humility in my own prayers.

Moses is my Bible crush. How could I not love a guy who got face-to-face time with God? How could I not love a guy who prayed and saw God respond? Moses was a crier, and I am one too, but I like Moses' version better. I cry when life gets hard—usually to the ceiling or with chocolate or something carb-filled in hand. Moses cried out to God. In fact, when I searched my Bible for all the times Moses prayed, I was startled to not find the phrase. Was my online search broken? No, Moses just "cried out" instead of "prayed."

What's the difference? Desperation, maybe. The root word of many of Moses' prayers to the Lord means "to cry, cry out, call, cry for help."[3] I want to cry out in prayer like I absolutely need God and am lost without him. It's true, so why wouldn't I want to pray like that?

Numbers 12:3 says that "Moses was very humble—more humble than any other person on earth" (NLT). The most humble guy got the most face-to-face time with God. Could this be a coincidence? I don't think so. Humility and desperation are requirements for prayer.

Moses gets me excited to come humbly to this conversation. He helps me recognize that coming laid bare, with nothing to offer besides myself, is where I want to be. Why? Because when we come humbly, we leave more room for God. And I know for a fact that more of God is better than more of me in any equation.

Andrew Murray wrote that man's "chief care . . . is to present [himself] an empty vessel, in which God can dwell and manifest His power and goodness."[4] A few pages later, he continues the vessel metaphor: "Just as water ever seeks and fills the lowest place, so the moment God finds [men] abased and empty, His glory and power flow in to exalt and to bless. He that humbleth himself—that must be our one care—shall be exalted; that is God's care."[5]

Most humans see humility as such a weakness, but as believers, we see something different. Humility comes when I know that I should make room for God. Strength comes when I let him in and get to experience his goodness as a result.

My family has a picture-book version of Psalm 23, and

on the last page, paired with the words "and I shall dwell in the house of the LORD forever," is a picture of a little lamb perched on one of those gates where the top swings open. Behind him is a watercolor torso—a man whose hands are placed on either side of the lamb. I wish you could visualize it with me now. That little lamb looks so at peace with his big God behind him. The lamb is small and quiet and not too powerful on his own, but he's got the equivalent of a superhero with him, so he's confident and content. That lamb had little to offer, much like Moses, yet he's dwelling in the house of the Lord and experiencing the Lord's abundance because he first decided to follow his shepherd and let him be Lord.

If you want to pray consistently, if you want to shake the weight of perfectionism and come to God with the right heart posture, get desperate. Scratch that. We don't need to *get* desperate; we already are. We just need to walk each day in the realization of who we are in relation to who God is.

2. Confess Often

The second necessary ingredient for praying with the right posture is confession. I skipped confession for much of my life, much like I did with studying humility. I was trying to get to the requests portion of the prayer conversation because I didn't want to run out of time for what I considered most important. And here's the thing: I was rushing to those requests only to have them not actually be heard.

I wonder how weary we've grown, lifting up the same requests to ears that aren't hearing them. Not because God ignores us but because of our willful choices to foster sin in our hearts. Psalm 66:18 tells us, "If I regard iniquity in my heart, the Lord will not hear me" (KJV).

These are strong words. Are we hearing right? Maybe this is out of context?

Nope.

"Regard" (translated as *cherished* in the ESV) means "to see, look at, inspect, perceive, consider."[6] Those sins we see and continue, the willful choices we make—the ones we consider and decide to do anyway? These "cherished" sins create a distance in our prayer lives, and God will not hear our prayers. Evelyn Christenson, author of *What Happens When Women Pray*, defines "regard" and its effects like this: "If we are living in sin and liking it, if we are keeping it there, finding that it feels kind of good, if we're regarding—nurturing, patting that little sin along—God does not hear us."[7]

This idea feels so wrong coming from a loving God. We interpret it to mean that he has stepped away because he can't handle our sin—like we're too disgusting or something. But let's keep digging into Scripture. The New Testament has some words on confession that we cannot miss.

Take James 4:8. We love to quote the first part of the verse, which says, "Draw near to God, and he will draw near to you." I've done it myself. But here's what the second part says: "Cleanse your hands, you sinners, and purify your hearts, you double-minded." If we long to draw near to God, we absolutely need to be cleansing our hands and purifying our hearts before him. This doesn't mean *we* actually do the cleaning. It means we acknowledge our mess before the Lord and give him access to it so we can be reconciled to him.

While unconfessed sin is clearly going to hinder a deep prayer life with the Lord, it's also going to wreak havoc on our hearts. David writes, "For when I kept silent, my bones wasted away through my groaning all day long. For day and night your hand was heavy upon me; my strength was dried up as by the heat of summer" (Psalm 32:3-4). Holding on to unconfessed sin as a believer is living an oxymoronic life. Of course there will be turmoil in our very beings.

Why would we desire to spend time with a wholly good God (and even get annoyed when he seems unresponsive) when we're purposely acting against what he stands for? If we are cherishing sin in our hearts and willfully disobeying God, even simple logic tells us our conversations with him will be strained.

As I've begun to value confession, I've noticed it's created a more humble spirit in me. It's always weird to call yourself humble, no? But really, when I've found myself judging someone in my thoughts, before I even finish, I notice and say, "Lord, forgive me! I shouldn't have thought that!" Understanding how sin hinders my conversation with the Lord is activating in me a posture of confession that I walk in throughout my day, not just during a ten-minute segment of my morning prayer time.

tip

Not sure how to start with confession? Take a few minutes to examine your day and ask the Lord to reveal your thoughts, words, attitudes, and actions that did not honor him. Express your sorrow over your sin and ask for his forgiveness. Try praying through Psalm 139:23-24:

Search me, God, and know my heart;
    test me and know my anxious thoughts.
See if there is any offensive way in me,
    and lead me in the way everlasting.
NIV

If confession still leaves you feeling more paralyzed than excited, I get it. Who wants to draw attention to his or her flaws? Doesn't that bring some amazing prayers down a few pegs? The reality is that confession brings God glory because it reveals truth and becomes an opportunity for him to forgive. Hidden sin doesn't bring glory to God. We might believe having it exposed makes us dirty or less worthy to speak to the Lord, but confessing our sin actually draws us closer to God.

We don't have to overcomplicate this. As we sit down to talk with the Lord, we can take a few minutes to humble ourselves, see what sins we've committed, and confess them to God. You want to talk about a humble heart posture? What do you think it says to the Lord when you come to him without fear, openly admitting the things you'd gladly keep hidden from the world? What do you think it says when you don't pridefully attempt your own cleansing but bring it before the one and only Redeemer?

Blessed by Brokenness

I'm stunned by a question pastor Ronnie Floyd asked: "When was the last time we were broken with grief over our own sins and alienation from our heavenly Father?"[8] Grieve over them? Most days I barely notice them.

Confession leads me to brokenness, and this brokenness snaps me back to eternal reality. It humbles me and reminds me who I am without God. This brokenness prepares my heart for absolute surrender.

What freedom we find when we come to terms with the sins we've ignored or tried to downplay for so long. We don't do ourselves or God any favors by rationalizing what we have done.

27

Do you feel bound up? Wound up? Angsty just talking about sin? Freedom awaits.

Selah.

As I've made confession a more consistent part of my prayer life, I now find myself sighing as I sit down to confess. It's not a Charlie Brown sigh but one of sheer relief that I no longer have to carry these weights on my own.

The enemy will attempt to make confession feel too heavy to even be worth it. Don't listen. God's mercies are fresh every morning. Keep confessing because until we get to heaven, we will sin. Our times of confession don't surprise God.

We will mess up in all aspects of life—including prayer.

We will choose the most ridiculous, should-be-an-easy-*no* distraction instead of time in prayer. We will stop praying because we had to Google what the weather would be that day . . . three feet from the front door. We will stop praying because we overslept after a late night of doing . . . absolutely nothing. We will stop praying because our friend said prayer didn't work for her and we thought, *Who am I to figure this out, then?* We will pray selfishly for all our pain to go away no matter who else it hurts. We will pray for hunter-green Saturns.

We aren't going to shock God. He knows our going and our coming.

We will fail. But if we can operate with humility and confession, we can keep returning to the Father in love. When we keep pride on retainer, it destroys our intimacy with the Lord. It's impossible to be intimate with him when we let linger any belief that we can win God over with just our performance and none of that demeaning grace. We'll save God the trouble and just power through in our own strength.

Besides that being theologically impossible, we will mess up and be left feeling like we can't go to God. We assumed he wanted us clean, which was great when we kept it together, but now we can't possibly come to him.

Psalm 139 comes to mind again. (I know what you're thinking: *This psalm? Twice in two chapters? C'mon!*) It's true. Because the Word is alive and active:

> O LORD, you have searched me and known me!
> You know when I sit down and when I rise up;
>   you discern my thoughts from afar.
> You search out my path and my lying down
>   and are acquainted with all my ways.
> Even before a word is on my tongue,
>   behold, O LORD, you know it altogether.
> You hem me in, behind and before,
>   and lay your hand upon me.
>
> PSALM 139:1-5

This time, it's what David says next in verse 6 that blows me away: "Such knowledge is too wonderful for me; it is high; I cannot attain it."

You know why I think David considered it so hard to grasp all that God knew about him? It certainly wasn't because he was perfect. You remember the infidelity with Bathsheba and calling the hit job on her husband, right? No, I think David found it wonderful to be fully seen by God and still be wholly loved. It wasn't just the being known but the being loved in spite of what God knew.

God knows everything about you, every bit of information you'd like to sweep under the rug and keep hidden. He knows it and still loves you. Why would we ever need to fear confessing to such a God?

Romans 5:8 says, "But God shows his love for us in that while we were still sinners, Christ died for us." If we worry about how we're coming off to God, spoiler alert—things aren't looking good for us. But if we get to see the reality of who God is—that his love for us isn't based on our flawless performance and that he knows vastly more about us than we'd ever share on a résumé or dating profile—we get to ease into his presence unencumbered by how we will look to him.

The Lord knows the posture of our hearts (see Jeremiah 17:10) and invites us to come near him anyway. That just might be all the reason we need to keep coming back to him in prayer.

3. Have Faith

James 1:6-7 says this about those who ask the Lord for wisdom: "Let him ask in faith, with no doubting, for the one who doubts is like a wave of the sea that is driven and tossed by the wind. For that person must not suppose that he will receive anything from the Lord."

I have been tossed by that wind before. At one point in my life, I was saying all the right things, but I didn't believe them. They were empty words that could have been coming out of any old ventriloquist dummy. No heart at all. Just hollowness.

If you'd asked me whether I believed, I would have told you yes. If you'd heard me pray, you would have assumed I believed too. But somehow, while I was saying all the right things, I was fixing my eyes on the circumstances. I put more belief in what I saw than in what I could not see: God.

I still see this creep up in the things that trigger my anxiety most. What's that fear that rattles your bones? The one that swirls your thoughts and makes it hard to remember truth? Mine always seems to relate to my health. A chest pain that's a result of heartburn attempts to tower over God in my mind when I start playing the game of "what ifs." *What if this time it's* not *heartburn but a heart attack? My family does have a history of it. I don't work out like I probably should. Yep, it's definitely a heart attack.* And just like that, I've put all my faith in circumstances I can touch and see instead of in God.

I've been working on capturing these thoughts and quickly reminding myself of a God who is very much alive. And, friend, it's working! When I stop to really think about God's power, ability, and desire to see me experience his peace, I am able to pray with conviction and faith.

We can talk about removing weights and learning new habits for prayer, but our methods don't matter one lick if we do not believe God is who he says he is.

Do we even believe God can do what he says he can do?

Do we even believe our prayers make any difference to the God of the universe?

Do we even believe our circumstances can change by simply speaking words in the air?

A handful of words in Mark 6 speak profoundly to this. Jesus went back to his hometown, and as he taught in the synagogue, people were essentially in disbelief that he had any authority to teach. *Oh, that's just Mary and Joseph's boy!* They only believed in what they saw. Mark tells us, "He could not do any miracles there, except lay his hands on a few sick people and heal them" (Mark 6:5, NIV).

The Amplified Version explicitly says, "He could not do a miracle there at all [because of their unbelief] except that He laid hands on a few sick people and healed them." There's no beating around that bush. The people's lack of faith stopped miracles from happening.

What are we missing out on simply because we don't believe God can do it?

What are we missing out on simply because we don't believe God can do it? If healings were minimized as a small footnote of what God had planned in Nazareth, holy cow! What level of miracles has unbelief kept from us today?

I love that mustering up more faith isn't all on us. Of course we will have doubts that we need to address with the Father, but for now, know this: If we want more faith, our first prayer should echo the disciples' words to the Lord in Luke 17:5: "Increase our faith!" And then we must believe he can do it!

When we throw off the weight of perfectionism, we can experience a deeper prayer life that's no longer paralyzed by coming "the wrong way" to prayer. We can come humbly, allowing our eyes to rest on the Lord instead of being consumed with what we bring to prayer. We can confess the real things that separate us from God—the big boulders of pride and other sin—and stop being tripped up by the pebble in the road—the specifics of how we pray—that seems to get most of our attention. We can spend more time falling in love with who God is and how worthy he is of our faith than being distracted by our doubts and secret attempts to solve problems on our own.

If we truly have a wrong heart posture, we won't "fix" it on our own. Coming to God in prayer knowing that he's the only one who can do something is humble and faith filled. If we can keep going to God, giving him access to our mess, we can experience prayer that leads to deep intimacy with our Creator.

reflect

What fears do you have about how you pray? Have you tried to solve them on your own?

How have these fears held you back in your prayer life?

How do you think you're supposed to pray? Does that align with what God tells us in his Word?

read

○ 2 Corinthians 12:9
○ Psalm 23
○ Hebrews 4:16
○ Titus 3:5
○ Hebrews 11:6
○ Romans 10:17

3

Will I Ever Get It?

Standing on God's Promises to Pray Confidently

LAST NIGHT WAS THE SCARIEST night of my life. We rode out Hurricane Sally, the slowest and most confused hurricane in the history of hurricanes, in a beach condo, fifteen stories up. It felt as if we were on a calm cruise ship. The sway wouldn't have been bad on the ocean, but in a building you hoped wouldn't crumble beneath you in a storm? It was terrifying. And Sally's two-mile-per-hour pace meant the torture lasted hours longer than any hurricane I've ever experienced in all my thirty-six years in southern Louisiana. As I followed the news, I almost had a panic attack when I read that Sally had strengthened to a Category 2 and shifted so it was on course to hit us right before making landfall. We were on a long-awaited beach trip with my parents and my siblings, but it's an understatement to say this was not the vacation I'd been hoping for. I was shaking like I was standing in subzero temps. Maybe *convulsing* is a better word.

My husband prayed over me. If I can be honest, I didn't hear a word he said and went back to my regularly scheduled convulsing. A few minutes later, we could hear a fire alarm going off outside our condo. Scratch that. Tyler heard it. All I could hear was the howling wind, which sounded way too close to a tornado's train sound, in my opinion.

Tyler investigated and found two women around my age with babies and toddlers who were in the hallway trying to get away from the blaring alarm in their condos.* He suggested that they come stay in our room until someone could figure out their alarm. A short time later, at around 2 a.m., we found ourselves sitting in the living room with just a cellphone flashlight for illumination. It was Tyler, Vivi, and Vana; my sister and her husband; and our new friends, Emily, Kelly, Chad, Cameron, and their families. Two sisters on vacation with their children and also their parents. One of the husbands pastored a church, and the other was a camp leader.

While I lay awake earlier in the pitch black of night, unable to hear anything but the howling wind, I prayed for God to calm the storm. That didn't happen, but God met us in that moment as he promised us in his Word to do. As the storm swirled around us, we sat with the sweetest distraction in the dark living room, sharing our fears and "I can't believe this is happening" thoughts. I was no longer in my bed, alone with my wandering thoughts. Things seemed to get worse as we watched a fire ignite across the way and heard of other

---

*My husband has a nose like a bloodhound for anyone he can rescue. It's one of the things that I love most about him because it's so unlike me. On our way to our beach vacation, he spotted a woman in the Target parking lot who had a flat tire and changed it for her. I was too busy thinking about Chick-fil-A to notice. His tire-changing experience came in handy when we got our own flat tire on our way home from the trip.

condo windows blowing out because of the high winds. Yet I told our new friends what an answer to prayer they had been to me. The storm had not been calmed, but the bondage to terrified thoughts I'd felt while scrolling through the news had been broken as total strangers and fellow believers offered an unspoken reminder that God was in our midst. It was impossible to miss God's generous presence and response to us in that moment.

It wasn't like I took a magic pill that made me suddenly not worry anymore. Even as I sit here typing a few hours later, hoping to not eat up too much of my computer battery, the wind is still raging. I'm watching the ceiling-fan cords sway as if someone just pushed them. I'm listening to the windows rattle. This isn't over. But now I'm confident instead of convulsing. The hurricane is still unnerving, but I can't deny the Lord's presence.

This experience is a stark reminder that I want to be careful what I cling to in prayer.

When I read about prayer warriors from previous generations, I'm in awe of what looks like such relaxed assurance that God will hear and answer. Missionary Hudson Taylor was once on a ship destined to collide with a sunken reef if winds didn't help the ship change course. He felt led to pray for wind and did so, first with a few other men and then alone. While alone, he said he "had a good but very brief season in prayer, and then felt so satisfied that our request was granted that I could not continue asking." He left his room and told the first officer to raise the sail. The man, who was an unbeliever, scoffed, but after more prodding he noticed the wind, raised the sails, and helped bring the ship to safety.[1]

Taylor was so in tune with the Lord that he sensed the

moment he was done praying and when to act. Me? Some of my prayers have come out as whispers because I wasn't sure I should even have been praying them. Confidence is good, but aren't these guys a bit cocky to pray with such boldness? Are we *sure* this is the way to pray?

After all, the most confident prayer of my youth was my misguided prayer for that hunter-green Saturn. My confidence didn't translate to God answering—and for good reason, as we've talked about. So where does that leave us? What I've come to realize is that prayer warriors are confident in what they're praying because they know God's words and promises.

Is it even possible to come to a conversation with the all-knowing, all-powerful God of the universe and approach his throne with confidence? Who am I to pray with authority in my voice, sure of what I ask for?

This is the weight of hesitation.

We cannot pray with confidence if we don't know *what* God has promised.

I couldn't confidently pray for God to stop the hurricane. Yes, I know he's capable and I think we *can* pray for things like that, but praying for things I'm really not sure are in God's will doesn't stop the shaking. What stops the shaking is remembering that God has promised to be with me always. That I am seen by God.

Not every prayer topic is addressed in the Word, and some promises in the Bible are just for the person who originally received them from God. I'm amazed, though, at how many promises the Bible holds for me and how much confidence we can bring to the throne room of God when we anchor our prayers in those promises.

It would be interesting to examine our prayers and see

how many are based on nothing but hopes and wishes. Is it any wonder we feel so flippant about prayer? When we pray for smooth circumstances, happier days, and less stress, we're not even sure what we're saying is biblical. We're just throwing noodles at the wall to see if one will stick.

First John 5:14-15 says, "This is the confidence we have in approaching God: that if we ask anything according to his will, he hears us. And if we know that he hears us—whatever we ask—we know that we have what we asked of him" (NIV). We have confidence when we ask according to his will. I love what David Guzik said about this passage: "For each prayer request, we should mentally or vocally ask, 'What possible reason do I have to think that God will answer this prayer?' We should be able to answer that question from His Word."[2]

If I'm praying for someone to know that God listens and loves and responds, look out. Even though I can't tell you how everything will turn out, I can pray with passion and focus because I trust what I've read over and over in Scripture about God's love. I also know that God does not hear the prayers of those who have known, unconfessed sin or who are harboring unforgiveness. I know from reading the history of mankind in my Bible that God loves us unconditionally. I don't know what that love will look like in every situation, but I know it's present. And I don't know why hard losses happen, but I know they don't negate what I am sure is true about God.

These are some of the things I know. They've shaped how I pray and how confidently I pray.

Thirteen-year-old me had the confidence, but she sure didn't have the wisdom. So how do we get to a place of confidently praying "the right things"? Here are five thoughts to help develop our confidence.

1. Remember It's a Process

If you're new to a relationship with Jesus Christ, you may feel overwhelmed and think that you need to prove yourself to God. Thankfully, that's not how it works. In 1 Corinthians 3:2, Paul says, "I gave you milk, not solid food, for you were not yet ready for it. Indeed, you are still not ready" (NIV). There's a learning curve to the life of faith and to prayer, but as we grow, we should move on to solid food.

If we're feeling stagnant in prayer, is it possible our confidence hasn't grown because we're still on a small supply of milk? Might it be because the only Scriptures we read are quick, pithy passages to help us in a crisis, verses a friend posts on social media, or what our pastor reads during his sermon on Sunday? All good things, mind you, but these can't be our only times in the Word. When we're not being fed by Scripture, our prayer lives will tend to center on our own immediate needs and feelings.

One meta thing we need to pray about is that God will reveal to us in his Word what we should pray about. Practically, this is my prayer sandwich. When I sit down to read my Bible, I start with a short prayer asking God to give me wisdom. This is so important because often I can plop on my couch and reach for my Bible as I would for a great self-help book. This is the Holy Word of God, though, and praying before I open it sets my mind on that truth. As I read a passage, that prayer also helps me tune my ear to the Lord's promptings, being careful to not insert what will tickle my ears (see 2 Timothy 4:3).

Reading a passage like Psalm 23:1-3 makes way for some really sweet prayers: "The LORD is my shepherd; I shall not want. He makes me lie down in green pastures. He leads me beside still waters. He restores my soul. He leads me in paths of righteousness for his name's sake." *Lord, I am weary, and you have said in your Word that you are my shepherd and you restore my soul. Restore me, Lord, and lead me into righteousness for your glory alone. I cannot do it without you. In Jesus' name, amen.*

Our prayer lives will grow in confidence *if* we are growing into digesting first milk and then the solid food of Scripture. Confidence in prayer can't just come from our mommas. My own mom is the one I credit most with teaching me how to pray. I always say we went "early and often" to the Lord because I was seriously afraid of everything as a child. That "milk" got me started, but at some point, I had other awakenings in my prayer life. What I had learned in my youth wasn't enough to sustain me as I very anxiously carried my first baby in my belly. At that time, I moved on to mushed-up solid food and embraced varieties of Bible studies mixed with written prayers.

More learning.

More growth.

I tackled reading through the Bible in a year on my own and enjoyed the fruits of small bites.

My growth continues even now as I dive deeper into theology and study.

I hope by the time I head home to heaven, I'll be dining on the perfectly sous vide filet mignons that are as rich and filling as it gets.

2. Remember It's for God's Glory

You want to see God move in your life? Who will get the glory if he does? When I was reading through the Bible most recently, I was amazed by the number of references to answered prayers and great acts of God that were tied to God getting glory. He performs miracles so people will know and believe he is God.

What type of miracles are you praying for right now? For your spring allergies or sore back to be healed? For your child to do better in school or for you to get a raise? If God said yes to any of these, would anyone know outside your family? Or would the answers be tucked inside and hidden? Would you forget that it was a God thing and chalk it up to coincidence?

We'd like to think God doesn't need a bigger reason to act than our own joy, right? God is beyond generous to us, but sometimes we think we're entitled to cushy lives. We think life is supposed to be easy, and if it's not, something is definitely wrong or maybe God doesn't even exist. We discount so much of what God does in our lives because of unreasonable expectations that have nowhere been promised to us.

We weren't promised a steady paycheck.

We weren't promised to be known and respected by people.

We weren't promised peace among nations.

We weren't promised free everything.

We weren't promised sunny vacations. (Still bitter about that hurricane.)

We completely forget the big picture when we're consumed by what we don't have instead of seeing the full story of the gospel we get to be a part of.

Here's just a quick sampling of some miracles, answered prayers, signs, and wonders discussed in the Bible, plus the correlation to God's glory. These miracles happened so that people would know and believe God. Let it blow you away for a few minutes.

Who gets the glory?

- Exodus 8:22—During the plagues, there were no swarms of flies where the Israelites lived so that they would know God is God.

- Exodus 14:4—God would gain glory through the Israelites' escape from Pharaoh and his army.

- Exodus 14:30-31—When the Israelites saw the parting of the Red Sea, they feared God and put their trust in him.

- Exodus 16:6-8—God gave the Israelites quail and manna to eat to show them he was the one who brought them out of Egypt.

- Exodus 20:2—God reminded the Israelites that he brought them out of slavery so they would remember his authority before he laid out the Ten Commandments.

- Joshua 4:23-24—God dried up the Jordan River so that the Israelites might know he was mighty.

- Daniel 2:24-47—Daniel was able to know and interpret King Nebuchadnezzar's dream, and the king acknowledged God as "God of gods and Lord of kings."

- Daniel 4:34—Nebuchadnezzar shared how his sanity was restored and how he immediately gave God the glory.

- Daniel 5:18-23—Daniel gave God glory for Nebuchadnezzar's greatness.

- Matthew 15:30-31—Jesus healed many people, and the crowd gave God the glory.

- John 14:13-14—Jesus said he will do what you ask in prayer so "that the Father may be glorified."

- Acts 2:1-11, 19-22—On the day of Pentecost, the people in Jerusalem from all around the known world heard the disciples sharing God's wonders in their own languages. Then Peter quoted the prophet Joel and talked about God doing signs and wonders so that people would be saved.

- Acts 3:1-12—Peter gave God the glory after he and John were able to heal a lame man.

When God moves in your life, what will your next move be? Will you praise him and give him glory? Or will you make mention of how hard you worked for whatever happened?

Selah.

Luke 16:10 comes to mind: "One who is faithful in a very little is also faithful in much, and one who is dishonest in a very little is also dishonest in much." Are we faithful to bring God glory with the small answered prayers, or are we waiting on the big miracles to shout from the rooftops?

I don't think this is a string we pull with God, like I praise God more so he'll do more. God knows our hearts. But I wonder if God works more in the lives of those he knows will sincerely give him the glory. If God's goal is to bring himself glory, doesn't it stand to reason that he will act in the lives of those who *will* point to him instead of those who plan to keep answered prayers to themselves . . . *if* they even notice that God has acted? If you've been in church very long, you've heard it said that God doesn't look for the most qualified. He looks for willing and ready hearts. Are we willing and ready to bring God the glory? If so, I think we'll be blown away by how God invades our lives when we pray with confidence.

3. Remember God's Character

I love the story of the second time God parted a body of water. This one's not quite as well known as the Red Sea incident, and it comes in Joshua 3 when the Israelites are crossing the Jordan River to get to the Promised Land. Verse 13 reads, "And when the soles of the feet of the priests bearing the ark of the LORD, the Lord of all the earth, shall rest in the waters of the Jordan, the waters of the Jordan shall be cut off from flowing, and the waters coming down from above shall stand in one heap."

> My faith isn't in predictable circumstances but in a consistent, unchanging God.

I love this because it reminds me to see God's past faithfulness not as a blueprint for what he will do in the future but as a reminder of *who* I'm trusting. My faith isn't in predictable circumstances but in a consistent, unchanging God.

The first time God parted the waters (see Exodus 14), Moses lifted up his hands and the water parted before the Israelites stepped in. The second time, the dry ground appeared only after the priests had stepped in the water. If I were Joshua, I'd be thinking, *God, aren't you going to clear the water first? I can lift my hands like Moses did if needed.* I might even think, *I guess my prayer didn't work. There's still water.*

The priests stepped in, though, and they saw God part the water just as he had back in Egypt.

After the parting of the Jordan, Joshua talked to the people about the purpose of the stones they had just arranged by the river. In verse 24, he said the stones were "so that all the peoples of the earth may know that the hand of the LORD is mighty, that you may fear the LORD your God forever."

The Israelites were about to go to battle for the land God had promised them. He needed them to know that he was worthy of all their trust. It's as if God were saying, "This miracle is so you know you can trust me for what's ahead."

What has God done in your past that you need to recall right now in your present circumstances? What in life has you completely forgetting his past faithfulness, and how can you walk forward in confidence remembering that the same God is with you now?

I cannot tell you how many times I've encouraged people to remember answered prayers. But even more than that, we need to remember the *character* of the God who answered those prayers. That's what will give us confidence to keep praying.

4. Remember to "Prejoice"

That's not a typo. I'm just pretending it's a word. It means to rejoice *before* the results.

Larry Richards writes, "We can find as much joy in affirming what God will do as in naming the blessings He has already given us."[3] Imagine how much confidence "prejoicing" could bring to our prayers. Have you prayed so uncertainly that you walk off thinking, *I'll guess we'll wait and see?* What would it be like to get up from praying and feel confident not because you know the result but because you flooded your heart with gratitude at what was to come?

There's always going to be something we can bemoan about God's response. We're human, and discontentment is a fleshly attitude we can fall back into. We can wish God were doing more, or we can open our eyes to what he *is* doing. I think we'd be blown away if we truly understood what he promised us and compared it with what he actually gave us.

David praised God in the midst of trouble, but I also love what he wrote in Psalm 43:3-4:

We can wish God were doing more, or we can open our eyes to what he *is* doing.

"Send out your light and your truth; let them lead me; let them bring me to your holy hill and to your dwelling! *Then I will go to the altar of God, to God my exceeding joy, and I will praise you with the lyre, O God, my God*" (emphasis added). He essentially promised praise. He didn't know what God would do, but he knew that the results, whatever they were, would be by God's hand, and he was already prepared to praise God for them. Such confidence.

5. Remember to Receive It

As we cover everything in our lives in prayer, we gain confidence from knowing that whatever is to come has been brought to the Lord. If I pray for no sickness to invade my child's body, then when sickness does come, I can more confidently stand on the fact that this was an unavoidable part of God's will. It didn't happen because I neglected to ask God to remove it. I don't love what is happening, but I trust it has a purpose.

This is hard to talk about. How do we explain things that happen that we didn't pray over? We often tie these up with a nice bow, saying that they must have been God's will. While we can't deny that, we simultaneously have to remember that God tells us we do not have because we do not ask (see James 4:2-3). And telling us to ask isn't a one-off command in Scripture. Here are just a few examples:

If you abide in me, and my words abide in you, ask
whatever you wish, and it will be done for you.
JOHN 15:7

You did not choose me, but I chose you and
appointed you that you should go and bear fruit and
that your fruit should abide, so that whatever you
ask the Father in my name, he may give it to you.
JOHN 15:16

Truly, truly, I say to you, whatever you ask of the
Father in my name, he will give it to you. Until now
you have asked nothing in my name. Ask, and you
will receive, that your joy may be full.
JOHN 16:23-24

Truly, I say to you, whoever says to this mountain,
"Be taken up and thrown into the sea," and does not
doubt in his heart, but believes that what he says will
come to pass, it will be done for him. Therefore I
tell you, whatever you ask in prayer, believe that you
have received it, and it will be yours.
MARK 11:23-24

Ask, and it will be given to you; seek, and you
will find; knock, and it will be opened to you. For
everyone who asks receives, and the one who seeks
finds, and to the one who knocks it will be opened.
MATTHEW 7:7-8

Again I say to you, if two of you agree on earth
about anything they ask, it will be done for them
by my Father in heaven. For where two or three are
gathered in my name, there am I among them.
MATTHEW 18:19-20

Do you think God wants to make sure we really understand this or what? We can pray confidently, knowing God
has told us to ask. And if what we prayed would occur doesn't,
we can rest in knowing that we do not have because God has
something better in mind, not because we didn't ask.

As we wrap up this chapter on developing confidence
and taking off the weight of hesitation, imagine for a second what confident prayer looks like. Imagine praying and
knowing that God is going to do what you ask because
it is what he promised in Scripture. This is why knowing
the promises of God is such an important component of
prayer, as we've discussed before. Get your Bible out. Look
for promises.* Study them in context, and recognize which
ones are for all people and which are just for the person who
originally received them. And then throw off the weight of
hesitation, hold on to the promises, and pray with confidence, friend.

---

*Not sure where to start? We've got some helpful resources at valmariepaper.com/study. Or check out the
tip about God's promises on page 108.

reflect ———————————————————————————

How can you give God glory when you experience answers to prayer?

Where do you see hesitation in your prayer life?

Which of God's promises can you cling to as you begin to pray with more confidence?

read ———————————————————————————

- ○ James 4:3
- ○ Romans 8:26
- ○ James 1:5

- ○ 1 Thessalonians 5:16-18
- ○ Psalm 25:1-5

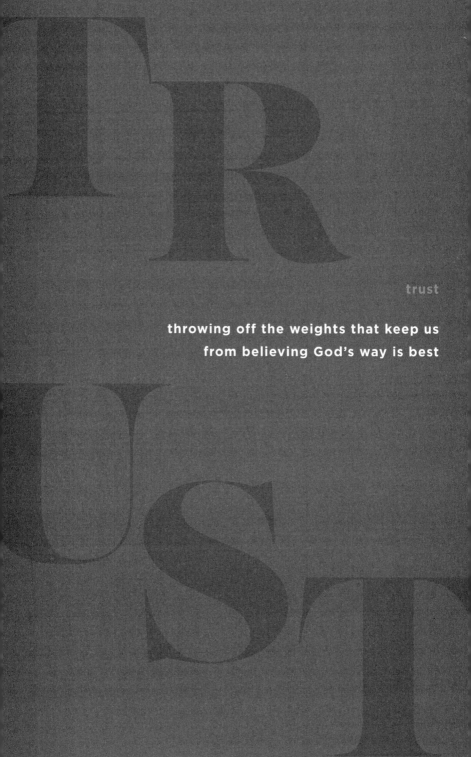

trust

**throwing off the weights that keep us
from believing God's way is best**

4

You Want It All?

Surrendering Every Part of Me

I REMEMBER IT LIKE IT WAS YESTERDAY, even though five years have passed. We sang "Overwhelmed" at the end of church one Sunday in August, and as I sang about delighting in the glory of God's presence, I was overwhelmed by how clearly God spoke to me.[1]

We were eight months into trying for our second baby. Each month when it didn't happen, I'd get disappointed and seek the Lord's comfort. I was sure this delay was his plan, but knowing that didn't eliminate my desire for a baby.

As we sang that morning, I felt the Lord speak more clearly than he's ever spoken to me—it was time to let go of my dream to have another baby.

I wasn't sure how to react at first. I had considered adoption before but assumed that if it happened, it would be after one more pregnancy. We had already started "trying," and to "stop trying" was hard for my efficient, to-do-oriented brain to comprehend. The plan was set in motion, and in my mind, to switch plans meant failure. I struggle just stopping a book in the middle, even if it's not that good.

I never in a million years thought I'd be able to say, "Okay, Lord. I give you this dream," but as the song played, I couldn't resist him. My heart was so totally matched with his plan for my life that I felt joy to give him this dream. I felt such a release as we left church: the most content I had ever been at the idea of maybe never being pregnant again. And I think that's right where I needed to be—fully surrendered, not clinging to this one thing.

I was far enough along in my cycle that I could have taken an early pregnancy test the very next day, but I decided to wait. I was finally content, plus I had a big product shoot later that week for our newest collection of prayer journals and didn't want to be consumed with a yes or no before the shoot. My birthday happened to be Friday, so I figured I'd take the test then, but I didn't tell anyone.

Friday morning, I popped out of bed and took the test. As soon as I saw the pink line, I walked out of the bathroom, leaving the test on the counter, and lay back in bed while Tyler headed in for his morning shower. When he saw the test, he started saying, "Seriously?" I was already in tears by this point, overjoyed by the good news. He hugged me and said it was pretty risky taking a pregnancy test on my birthday. What if it had been a no? I told him that I had felt so much peace about the outcome that, regardless of the response, I would have been okay that day.

That's a nice story, isn't it? Total surrender, with joy in the midst of it—and then in the end I get to keep what I just surrendered? Yeah, I want to punch me too.

Not every story of surrender ends wrapped with a festive bow, but what I learned from that season was something I never want to forget. Surrender of any kind requires being totally consumed with the Lord. When we can see only him, it becomes possible to surrender.

Want a less fairy-tale version of how I learned this lesson?

I deal with chronic pain, and I often ask my husband for prayer. At times he has worried that I pray in the hopes that it would serve as some sort of Band-Aid. He has wondered what was actually happening when we kept praying for things that seemed not to budge. I still faced chronic pain, and more often than not, it appeared that I prayed not to engage with our Creator but to put him on like a weighted blanket that momentarily made me feel better.

I completely got the concern. But so often, what looked like me seeking only comfort was actually me seeking the ability to surrender—something I couldn't do apart from God.

I told Tyler that when he prayed for me and my current ailment, it helped me surrender the situation to God. I wasn't always pining for a miracle when I came to pray (although I wouldn't turn one down). First and foremost, I came with a hope that my stubborn grip would loosen as he and I approached the throne room together. I wasn't closing my eyes and hoping the problem would leave me—although those aren't bad prayers. Jesus prayed for the cup to pass from him. Daniel, I have to imagine, prayed to not go in that lions' den. And some days I pray for miraculous healing. But before I can pray those prayers, I want to make sure I'm genuinely surrendering everything to God.

Surrender can draw us into God's presence like never before as we put our full trust in him. But when I keep my grip so tightly on what I want from God as I pray, I'm not learning to trust. That's still me rubbing a magic lamp looking for a genie to answer my wish.

If you're like many believers, you feel confident you're past the magic-lamp phase of prayer. You understand surrender. You understand God's will. But my guess is that we all have some hidden parts of our lives where we'd prefer to hold the reins.

This is the weight of exceptions.

We miss out on a contentment that comes from fully trusting God when we make exceptions for certain things we're not ready to surrender.

When I fully trust God, I can release the tension in my chest that takes the shape of a balled-up fist no strongman could unclench. When I fully trust God, I can breathe, really breathe and relax. When I fully trust God, I can experience more joy because I'm not in a constant state of trying to make my plan happen. I can experience contentment instead.

You know the difference between taking a trip where you've planned out every detail and taking a trip where you're just riding shotgun? Sometimes we want the control, but have you ever experienced going along for the ride without a worry in the world? You know you're not in charge, so you just follow the person with the itinerary. There's something freeing about that.

Imagine if we prayed like that.

Imagine if we *lived* like that.

No matter how good we are at surrender, we each hold on to something in our lives. It feels small and almost like our consolation prize for giving up so much to God. *God, I'll give you my career but not my search for a husband. I can't have anything going wrong with that one. What if I throw in the city I live in, the friends I make, and even how many kids I have? That's a ton for you to work with! I know you'll do great! But yes, I'm still gonna hold on to that husband search. If you want something done right, you have to do it yourself . . . right?*

The small thing I keep feels like the reward for all I've given to God. What a faithful little believer I am to give God so many parts of my life. Am I the only one who thinks so arrogantly about surrender? I think I'm doing God a favor to give up so much, completely neglecting the fact that full and total surrender is the greatest place to be.

That one thing we keep holding on to, whether big or small, reveals our lack of trust in God.

> That one thing we keep holding on to, whether big or small, reveals our lack of trust in God.

The big things we hold back reveal what we're too scared not to control. The small things we hold back reveal what we don't think God would bother with anyway. Keeping hold of anything won't serve us or our prayer lives.

Selah.

Take a few minutes right now and consider: What's that last thing you'd imagine releasing your grip on? Ask the Lord to reveal what in your life has been the hardest for you to surrender. What makes it difficult to release? What did you fear would happen if you did let go?

That God would forget?

That God would get greedy and ask even more of you?

That God would try to teach you a lesson?

That last one gets me a lot. I'm scared that if I surrender my family, he'll take it from me. (Perhaps that's why my prayer of surrender for a second pregnancy was so earth shattering. It was literally my greatest fear to give that up to God.) My sister, in a Bible study she wrote, said we can feel like "God was just looking for someone naive enough to hand [their dream] over, that He could take up on their offer, because no one else was willing to do it."[2] Have you ever felt that way before?

Here's the truth: My lack of surrender won't prevent occurrences that I want to avoid. God is too strong, and I am too weak. Not surrendering just means the process is more painful because whatever I can't release must be pried out of my hands.

Sometimes we're holding on to our one thing so tightly that it almost feels as if it's keeping us safe—like we trust it instead of God. Remember the story of Peter walking on water when Jesus called to him (see Matthew 14:22-33)? Imagine that you're in a boat and God is asking you to step out and walk to him. You're leaning over the edge telling God you trust him, but you've got five life preservers attached to you. When you lean forward, your trust is in the five life preservers, not in the invisible God. Then imagine telling God, *Look, I'll remove all the life preservers and just keep this one. Isn't it better than if I'd kept all five? I just want to keep this one tiny thing. It's no big deal! I mean, it can barely hold me. I'm really having to rely on you anyway, God. What does it hurt?*

Having one life preserver instead of five might look better, but the reality is we've just sunk a lot of trust into that one we kept around. Our one thing carries so much weight. Did you give up everything for that dream job and now the pressure for it to be perfect is suffocating? Did you sink your life savings into IVF and this is literally your one shot for a biological baby? Did you move across the country because your boyfriend was supposed to propose soon and now your relationship feels like it's in a pressure cooker?

It's hard not to put all our trust in that one life preserver. We're not able to hold on to something casually. If we've chosen to give up everything but one thing, its grip on us will steal intimacy in our prayer lives.

True surrender requires intense faith, and if we want to experience the trust that comes from surrendering everything, we can't hold on to anything. We can't be partially surrendered. It's an oxymoron.

So what does it look like to surrender everything? And how do we pray about things we've surrendered? How do we ask while simultaneously releasing the results? How can we pray when our hearts aren't saying, "Your will be done" but instead are asking, "Lord, do you mind if my will be done this time?"

1. Decide Whether You Can Trust God

If God can't be trusted with everything, he can't be trusted with anything. If you believe God sent his Son to die on the cross to pay for our sins so that we'd experience life in heaven with him instead of eternity separated from him, can't you trust him with your health, your future mate, or your wayward teen?

Maybe we should back up a bit.

Salvation in itself requires us to surrender to God. If giving everything to God in prayer doesn't feel necessary to us, maybe we misunderstand what it means to follow Jesus.

To be honest, it wouldn't be difficult in today's age of the prosperity gospel, which hits pretty hard on what we get from God without addressing what God requires of us. In Matthew 16, Jesus tells his disciples:

> If anyone would come after me, let him deny himself and take up his cross and follow me. For whoever would save his life will lose it, but whoever loses his life for my sake will find it. For what will it profit a man if he gains the whole world and forfeits his soul? Or what shall a man give in return for his soul?
> VERSES 24-26

There is a cost to trusting God, but what we gain is significantly greater than what we lose. God has proven himself worthy of all our trust, but we may need to dig into what that actually means for our lives.

My twin sister, Natalie, needed a dogsitter for her dog, Baxter, and I suggested the babysitter who watches our daughters. Now you have to understand the relationship my sister has with this dog. Baxter arrived on a red-eye flight from the Ukraine about two hours before the airports shut down because of COVID-19. Natalie has spent the last several months hunkered down at home and not leaving him alone, so this was a big step. She teased, "Do you think I can trust your babysitter to take Baxter for walks?" I said, "Well, I trust her to walk my girls, sooooo . . . yeah." We both laughed because my answer highlighted how silly her question was, but I think we do that with God, too. We trust him for our salvation but aren't sure we can trust him with our career paths.

So talk it out with God, even if it sounds ridiculous. Acknowledge what you do trust him with and what you're on the fence about, and listen to the words as you say them. Many times, what seems like a great struggle gets sifted when we name it.

I'm confident you can trust God with everything, but we each need to come to that conclusion for ourselves. If you've never done that, don't wait. What you believe about God—how trustworthy you consider him—is foundational to your prayers.

2. Remember That It's Personal

Psalm 81 describes God calling the Israelites to listen and submit to him. As you read the passage below, feel the emotion of God's words. He had saved his people from slavery and settled them in a wonderful land—and yet they were still ignoring his teaching and following idols. You're not an Israelite, but you are God's adopted child. He's calling us to listen to him, to submit everything to him.

> Hear, O my people, while I admonish you!
>   O Israel, if you would but listen to me!
> There shall be no strange god among you;
>   you shall not bow down to a foreign god.
> I am the LORD your God,
>   who brought you up out of the land of Egypt.
>   Open your mouth wide, and I will fill it.
>
> But my people did not listen to my voice;
>   Israel would not submit to me.
> So I gave them over to their stubborn hearts,

> to follow their own counsels.
> Oh, that my people would listen to me,
>   that Israel would walk in my ways!
> PSALM 81:8-13*

This passage is heartbreaking because somehow I can convince myself that God didn't really intend for this call to surrender to apply to *me*. I know he asks me to follow him, but surely when I fall behind a few paces, he doesn't notice that I'm still lugging a few things I have deemed essential.

I can't picture him saying, "If you would but listen to me, Valerie!" I can't picture him saying, "Valerie would not submit to me . . ." or "Oh, that Valerie would listen to me and walk in my ways!" But as I read this passage, I start to see the seriousness of holding on to what God is calling me to submit.

Where are we, like the Israelites, ignoring what God has done in our lives and forgetting that trusting him brings the best outcomes?

This sounds heavy, and it is, but it's also hope-filled. Don't Charlie Brown—walk your way to surrender with your head hung low, kicking the dirt as you go. Run to God. I know that may not be easy, but I promise it will be good.

3. Share Your Heart

It's possible to send up requests to the Big Guy while still trying to conceal our hearts and hold back what we're not

---

*We'll talk in chapter 7 about how God won't respond to our requests that aren't a part of his will. But didn't he just do that in Psalm 81? Not exactly. It wasn't that the Israelites were asking God to let them wander away and he said yes. It doesn't seem like they were asking him anything at all. This verse and several others (see Deuteronomy 29:18 and Jeremiah 3:17; 7:24; 23:17) refer to people acting willfully against God's commands and to God allowing them to follow their own way and suffer the consequences—all while continuing to love them and call them back. Praying for something and hoping that God will say yes is very different from defiantly pursuing your own way.

ready to surrender. But what if we saw praying less as asking for things and more as *sharing our hearts* with God?

Think about the intimacy of that statement. In that paradigm, we are no longer dissecting what God gets access to in our lives. We're not deciding what he can handle. We're not picking what to delegate. We're spending more time handing over our whole hearts, focusing on him rather than focusing on the issues that weigh us down.

I'm amazed at the amount of time I spend not really praying but reviewing the facts in a way that doesn't require God's presence at all. It's navel-gazing, which the Oxford English Dictionary defines as "self-indulgent or excessive contemplation of oneself or a single issue, at the expense of a wider view."[3] What's the wider view? How God fits into this whole thing.

When we instead share our hearts with God, the emphasis is on him, and we stop the excessive solitary contemplation of what we'll share and what we won't. We just give God access to it all.

4. Hold the Outcome Loosely

Sharing our hearts is the prerequisite to surrender because we have to acknowledge what we're giving to God. If we don't, we get whiplash because we weren't ready to let it go, and we'll try to grab it back. When we've named what we're surrendering, we make our requests known to the Lord and leave the outcome to him, staying limber and alert for what is next. When we hold the outcome loosely in our hands, we aren't placing our open hands, holding something so precious to us, over the pits of hell. Our hands are over the Lord's hands. If we release something, he catches it. The invisible nature of God makes surrendering feel riskier than it actually is.

We're tactile people who believe in what we can touch with our own hands and see with our own eyes, so we often want to pull back from what we can't see. This is why prayer is so important. Yes, God is invisible, but as we pray, we get to see him move. We get to see his invisible hand changing our hearts, our circumstances, and the world around us. I've watched cartoons with my girls where a character will make himself invisible and then we'll see a cup move off a table or a door open, seemingly on its own. We know the character is there because of what he is doing. In the same way, prayer is our way of seeing an invisible God at work all around us.

> **Prayer is our way of seeing an invisible God at work all around us.**

I pray that this knowledge encourages you to trust God and surrender everything to him. Keep your eyes open to see where God is moving, which will remind you that the hands you have put your trust in are real.

Here's what holding something loosely has looked like for me before: *Lord, I feel you are calling me to _____. It scares me. I want to do your will. I know your plan is good, but here's what's weighing on me. _____ Would you reconcile these weights with your will? Would you remove the unrest I feel if I need to step forward? I'm willing but shaky. Make me strong.*

5. Stay Soft

Surrendering isn't a one-time process. Throughout our lives, we'll find new things that feel too scary to pass off to the Lord. The best way I know to prepare for them is to stay soft. Do what David did when he said in Psalm 139:23-24, "Search me, O God, and know my heart! Try me and know my thoughts! And see if there be any grievous way in me, and lead me in the way everlasting!"

With this prayer, we invite the Lord to make us aware of our missteps. It's the opposite of trying to conceal things and keeping a death grip on what we want. As we do this, we'll be strengthening our muscles of surrender and growing in our faith and trust in the Lord. Imagine the prayers we will pray in such a state!

———————

When we throw off the weight of exceptions and fully surrender all we have to God, we reap the benefits of contentment and fully trusting in our Father.

I'll close with a few lines from a hymn that is placed on my stubborn heart in moments I want to control. Even though I haven't sung this song in church in ages, my heart knows how I need to respond in the moment, and these words help me get there.

All to Jesus I surrender,
Make me, Savior, wholly Thine.
Let me feel Thy Holy Spirit,
Truly know that Thou art mine.

I surrender all, I surrender all;
All to Thee, my blessed Savior,
I surrender all.[4]

reflect

Are there any circumstances still lingering that make you unsure whether you can trust God?

What thing currently feels impossible to surrender to God?

What promise do you need to meditate on that would help you surrender what you're holding on to?

read

- ○ Jeremiah 10:23
- ○ Proverb 23:26
- ○ Luke 9:23-24

- ○ Romans 12:1
- ○ Galatians 2:20

5

What If I Don't Feel Like It?

Letting Truth, Not Emotions, Determine My Obedience

HAVE YOU EVER PRAYED looking for a second opinion? You've exhausted all your resources and now you want to see what this big, powerful God would suggest. You're not sure if you're ready to obey, but you at least want to hear him out. *Hey, his ideas might actually be good!*

As absurd as that sounds, my actions (or lack thereof) perfectly illustrate that I've thought like this in the past. And I think it all started out innocently enough. The good girl in me spent lots of time trying to win God's love through obedience, and once I figured out that he loved me no matter what, I overcorrected hard. I saw obeying God as making some sort of payment, and that had no place in my story. "Grace" was the title of my rewrite. In my mind, obedience equaled legalism, so I was just going to focus on the heart.

We've spent time diving into our motives and the heart. That's, of course, where we need to start because everything else flows from it (see Proverbs 4:23). But want to know what flows from a *righteous* heart?

Obedience.

Obedience is hard to talk about, but in my experience, it plays a crucial part in both how we pray and how we view prayer. For example, when you pray, do you already have a loose outline of a plan and you're just hoping for clarity on the details and God's official stamp of approval? Are you praying with one eye closed, terrified of what God might tell you to do? Or do you pray ready to obey whatever God says next?

Our emotions (such as fear, anticipation, being overwhelmed—did I mention fear?) want to convince us that they should decide how we respond. If we're afraid of what God might tell us, we feel the tug to listen to the fear instead of overriding it and obeying God.

This is the weight of emotions.

We create distance and miss out on hearing God more clearly when we let emotions lead us into disobedience.

When I read *Discerning the Voice of God* by Priscilla Shirer, I was struck by how much she talked about obedience, weaving it throughout the book. It felt like an unexpected way to structure a book on prayer. In my mind, prayer and obedience looked like opposites. I thought you either prayed and *waited* or you obeyed and *did* something. One is active. The other is passive.

What I missed that we're going to drive home pretty strongly in this chapter is this: our prayer lives cannot thrive without obedience. Committing to follow God's direction rather than our own emotions is not an optional part of prayer that we add every now and then. To lead with our hearts, as the world tells us to do, is a road of destruction if our hearts aren't beating in sync with the one who created them.

Don't Ignore God

If we invite God to work in our lives but include more red tape than the IRS, let's not fool ourselves and wonder why our prayer lives aren't flourishing. They're not flourishing because God isn't the quintessential best friend in a rom-com. You know the one—she's reliable and listens, but she isn't the hero. She supports the protagonist and gives wise counsel, but if we're honest, we see that the protagonist only listens if it's what she wants to do anyway.

> We can't treat God like the best friend who gives advice that we have no plan to listen to.

We can't treat God like the best friend who gives advice that we have no plan to listen to. We can't treat God like this is our story and God's merely a prop to round out the cast of players. Our prayer lives can't flourish under such conditions. We jump to blame God for not speaking to us, but is there a chance that when he has spoken clearly, we've just tuned him out and done what we wanted anyway?

Disobedience will dull our ears to truth the same way Pharaoh hardened his heart toward God. Maybe you've read the Exodus account of Pharaoh seeing sign after sign that God was telling him, through Moses, to free the Israelites from captivity. You've read that, somewhere in that process, God hardened Pharaoh's heart, and it made you a little uncomfortable. Could God harden ours, too?

Pharaoh had a track record. Exodus 5:1-2 says, "Moses and Aaron went and said to Pharaoh, 'Thus says the LORD, the God of Israel, "Let my people go, that they may hold a feast to me in the wilderness."' But Pharaoh said, 'Who is the LORD, that I should obey his voice and let Israel go? I do not know the LORD, and moreover, I will not let Israel go.'"

The Bible Project broke down what happened after Pharaoh's first declaration of disobedience. These are his responses to the ten plagues that followed:

1. Blood: Pharaoh's heart "became hard" (7:22).
2. Frogs: Pharaoh "hardened his own heart" (8:15).
3. Gnats: Pharaoh's heart "was hard" (8:19).
4. Flies: "Pharaoh hardened his own heart" (8:32).
5. Livestock die: Pharaoh's heart "was hard" (9:7).
6. Boils: "The Lord hardened Pharaoh's heart" (9:12).
7. Hail: Pharaoh "hardened his own heart" (9:34).
8. Locusts: God announces that he has "hardened Pharaoh's heart" (10:1,10:20).
9. Darkness: God "hardened Pharaoh's heart" (10:27).
10. Death of the firstborn: God "hardened Pharaoh's heart" (11:10).[1]

The language in the first five plagues was either ambiguous or implied that Pharaoh hardened his own heart. The following five plagues state four times that God hardened Pharaoh's heart.

God is not the initiator of heart hardening. We are. Pharaoh may be an extreme example, but in his story, it's telling to see how much easier it gets to say no to God after we've already said no to God.

That's not the life I want.

I want a life that flows from rich prayers. It's easy to see prayers as just talking to the ceiling. We do our duty, and that's it. But our communion with the Lord has the power to direct us where to go if we're ready to obey what we hear. If every fear or selfish desire steers us in the opposite direction, though, we're missing out. We let shaky things like our own emotions determine what we will say yes to instead of deciding beforehand that we will obey the Lord before he ever lays out a full plan.

Pharaoh had a foil who did obey: Moses. Where Pharaoh exercised continuous disobedience and a hardening heart, Moses repeatedly obeyed God and continued to hear from him.* In just two chapters in Exodus, 39 and 40, the line "as the Lord had commanded Moses" is repeated fourteen times as Moses is given specific instructions about the Tabernacle and other rituals. Exodus nearly comes to a close with the line "So Moses finished the work" (Exodus 40:33).

I can't help but think about how Moses' time in God's presence affected his obedience. The more time we spend with the Lord, the more we understand his plans (with our still very limited brains) and trust that they are good.

As I read about the life of Moses, my passion for this personal relationship and "face time" with the Father intensifies. For Moses, it impacted everything. It impacted his relationships with those he led as he prayed and asked God to redeem them. It impacted his actions as he heard God's leading and followed his direction. The result was not an easy, comfortable life. (Moses did, after all, lead two million complainers on a forty-year trek in the wilderness.) But the fruit was vibrant. Radiant, even, as he got to spend incredible time in the presence of the Lord.

---

*One notable exception later in Moses' life is recorded in Numbers 20, when Moses relied on what had worked in the past and struck a rock to get water for the Israelites, instead of speaking to the rock the way God asked him to.

To the world, obedience can feel stifling because, obviously, we have our own plans and, obviously, doing someone else's is no fun. Truly, though, it's hard to read Moses' stories without seeing the beauty of obedience and yearning for the depth that comes when we keep saying yes to God. I don't think I'm telling you anything new when I say that the things we think are full of freedom, such as having our own way, don't bring actual freedom. It's in obedience that we experience God's plan for us.

Even in the Lord's Prayer we see an opportunity to prepare our hearts to obey the Father's will: "May your will be done on earth, as it is in heaven" (Matthew 6:10, NLT). It's the decision we make before we know the next step. It's communicating to the Lord that even though we don't have all the facts, even if we don't feel like it, we've decided we will obey. Not because we know it will be easy but because we trust the one who is instructing us.

YOUR will, Father, not mine. Those are hard words to come by sometimes.

Matthew 26:39 paints a picture of the Garden of Gethsemane, where Jesus sweated blood before he was betrayed and arrested: "And going a little farther [Jesus] fell on his face and prayed, saying, 'My Father, if it be possible, let this cup pass from me; nevertheless, not as I will, but as you will.'" Even Jesus felt the weight of his emotions. I don't think this will surprise you, but if I'd been in Jesus' shoes, about to be arrested, I likely would have let fear carry me faster than I've ever run before . . . away from the cross.

I'm currently teary-eyed in a coffee shop. I'm sad Jesus had to face such circumstances, but on top of that, I selfishly see the weight of those words—"not as I will, but as you will"—and fear what it could mean for me to say them myself. I fear the unknown of what it means to say I'll obey before I even know what that looks like.

This isn't a flippant choice we make or something we tack on to prayer in hopes that God will put us at the top of his "answer" list. This is a choice we make because of what we believe, which is why it's important that we laid a foundation in chapter 1 about who God really is.

Our choices to obey are based on Scripture. They're based on what we've seen God do in our lives or the lives of others around us. And I want to remember that no matter what obedience looks like in my life, it will always be better than hardening my heart, sacrificing intimacy with God, or experiencing the natural consequences that come when I disobey.

We so often isolate the hard things that require obedience without looking at the alternative. When we're choosing whether to obey God, the alternative isn't pretty—it involves hightailing it in a direction God didn't plan for us. The phrase "the safest place for me to be is in the center of God's plan" is one of those trite sayings that strikes a tender nerve for me. I like safety, and sometimes I have to be reminded where the real danger lies—not in the unknown of God's plan but in the seemingly "known" outside of God's plan.

Don't Stall

When someone asked George Mueller* what the most important part of prayer was, he reportedly said, "The 15 minutes after I have said, 'Amen.'"[2] What happens after we pray? If you're anything like me, you get up and go on your merry

---

*Mueller is known for establishing several orphanages in England and not asking others to provide for the children's needs but instead praying about them. He saw God provide in incredible ways due to his faith. If you want to read a biography of a prayer warrior, I highly recommend his.

way. There's a disconnect between our prayer lives and our real lives. Yep. I heard it too. The truth is our prayer lives *are* our real lives. But how often does our prayer time direct our next steps?

Want a semi-modern example of what it looks like for our prayer lives to direct our steps? I say *semi-modern* because I came across it in a book written before cell phones, Internet, and maybe color TV. The words that caught my attention were the least spiritual sounding words of the entire book, but they had me highlighting and taking notes. Here they are: "I'm taking Marion to lunch."[3]

The author, Evelyn Christenson, was part of a prayer group that had spent time praying and praying for the salvation of someone they knew, a woman named Marion. As they closed, Evelyn said those words to the group. I wrote in the margins, "Pray & Act."

Evelyn's whole story was overflowing with answered prayers and opportunities, and I can't help but assume it's because of this very sentence and many more like it. When God asked her to do something, she didn't hesitate.

I want the Lord to know that when he tells me something, I don't need sixteen fleeces to make sure I heard right. Have you heard the Old Testament story of Gideon asking for signs to make sure he understood God? It's not exactly a practice to model ourselves after. Gideon already had God's direction (see Judges 6:11-24), but he asked God to make a sheep's fleece wet to confirm what God was asking him to do. He told God in Judges 6:37, "I will put a wool fleece on the threshing floor tonight. If the fleece is wet with dew in the morning but the ground is dry, then I will know that you are going to help me rescue Israel *as you promised*" (NLT, emphasis added). After God did what he asked, Gideon asked him to do it again—but this time reversed, with the fleece dry and the ground wet.

Maybe Gideon was buying time, or maybe his faith needed to mature a little. He knew God had promised to rescue Israel, but he let his fear convince him that he needed more signs before he could move forward in obedience.

So how do we not let emotions hold us back when we pray and receive direction? We take the first step. We don't stall, because fear provides ample time for the world's logic to convince us we heard wrong.

> The more we sit back and wait for greater and greater signs, the more convinced we become that we can't move without them.

My own journal is full of decisions I've made but still held loosely just in case I heard God wrong. I pray for an unsettled spirit within me if I'm going in the wrong direction, but I think it's important to move, even with caution. The more we sit back and wait for greater and greater signs, the more convinced we become that we can't move without them. I remember a friend in college saying he wasn't going to propose to a girl until God told him to by writing it in the sky. That was the day my crush on him ended because I have an idea of how many times that's happened in the history of the world, and I want to say it's zero to none. I got the sentiment. He wanted to be sure. But I think so many times, the fear of not knowing for sure paralyzes us. If you've been in the research-and-development phase for far too long, maybe the culprit is fear of obeying rather than a God who's not being clear enough.

Recently we had an opportunity presented to us for our girls to homeschool with a retired teacher and one other family during this unprecedented 2020–2021 school year during COVID-19. Since we were facing lots of unknowns and deadlines, it sounded like it could be a great thing, but it would also be a big change and a big risk. I told the other mom I'd pray about it for three days, and my husband and I spent time fasting and praying. We also had several conversations, asked questions, talked about the possibilities, and weighed the pros and cons. By the end of three days, we felt comfortable it was the right thing. We didn't have that "100 percent, beyond a shadow of a doubt, this is it" feeling, but we felt solidly that God was leading us in that direction, and we made the decision. Over the following weeks and months, confirmation kept coming, and by the time school started, we knew it was the right decision beyond a shadow of a doubt.

If we had looked for 100 percent confirmation before we made a move, we wouldn't have moved. And maybe we'd have been kicking ourselves in those weeks that followed, when the COVID-19 restrictions shifted. Instead, my husband and I just looked at each other and thanked God we'd made the decision we had made.

If you're waiting for your whole path to be lit up with runway lights, you'll be waiting longer than my old crush from college waited to find the right woman. We know God doesn't light the entire path. We get just the next step. Know why I think that is? Because imagine how silly it would be if you asked for directions and some kind sir gave you a detailed map, telling you about all the twists and turns and mile markers. Then as you thanked him and started to leave, he said, "Wait, I'm coming with you." Wouldn't your reaction be, "Well, then, why did you give me all those directions if you're going to guide me personally?"

Doesn't it make more sense that we don't get the full story? The journey is intended to be walked with our guide. When we don't prioritize prayer and an intimate relationship with the Lord, it's like we're telling God we can go this road on our own with just a few instructions from him. What gives us such confidence? We don't have the map. We don't know the roads. We need God. That's always been true, but we forget it often.

Selah.

I want to walk so closely with the Lord that it's possible for me to pick his voice out of a crowd of lies. John 10:27 says, "My sheep hear my voice, and I know them, and they follow me." What dulls our ears to the voice of God is disobedience.

Obedience isn't an elective part of prayer. This isn't P. E. or shop class. (Sorry, P. E. and shop class.) If we long to hear God speak into our lives, we need to examine *how* we are responding to him and even *if* we are responding to him at all or are just waiting for another soggy fleece.

Repent and Try Again

If you've let emotions take control and have strayed from the Lord or disobeyed, let this be a moment of coming back to God and recommitting your heart to obedience.

In Genesis 31:13, God tells Jacob, who has lived with his Uncle Laban for many years, to return to the land where he was born. Jacob starts on the journey with his whole family and large herds of livestock but then parks his fanny where God didn't tell him to stop, in Shechem. Shortly afterward,

---

Prayer in action

Do you ever read a passage and think, Whoa, this is like a textbook *because the lesson is laid out so succinctly? As I was reading Genesis 24, about Abraham's servant traveling to the land of Abraham's extended family to find a wife for Abraham's son, Isaac, I saw that it's basically a sermon outline on prayer and obedience! Read the full chapter of Genesis 24 and see the findings below:*

1. Make prayer our first response, not our last resort (verses 10-12).

2. Pray specifically (verse 14).

3. Take a step forward to act. Sometimes when we *think* we heard God but aren't 100 percent positive, we wait for him to pick us up and move us. Instead, take action and also pray for an unsettled spirit or a closed door if you're moving in the wrong direction (verse 17).

4. Listen and get quiet so God can speak and confirm (verse 21).

5. Give God the glory. The servant worshiped God and then told Rebekah's family, "God led me." He gave God the credit (verses 26-27). How easy it is to keep answered prayers to ourselves.

---

there's an entire chapter (Genesis 34) filled with tragedy— the rape of Jacob's daughter, Dinah, and then the murder of her attacker by her brothers. It's a heavy story, but what struck me was that there was not one mention of God in the chapter.

I've got my theories. Maybe Jacob knew he'd disobeyed God by setting up shop in a land of worldly temptations. Maybe he felt too ashamed to run to the Lord for help.

Maybe the disobedience dulled his ears to God's voice, and prayer wasn't even a thought. Regardless, he didn't turn to God in the midst of it.

In Genesis 35:1, God tells Jacob to go to Bethel, and this time Jacob listens. He tells his family to get rid of their idols and essentially turns back to God. He even receives a new name and identity: Israel. Within this chapter, God is mentioned eleven times. Looked at side by side, these chapters illustrate how sin separates us from God as well as how much our obedience is strengthened by our ability to hear him and vice versa.

We spend a lot of time looking for clarity and seeking wisdom, but God has already promised to give wisdom generously (see James 1:5). The question is, what will we do with it? Can we stop overanalyzing the job God is doing as he gives us the next step and instead pay close attention to how we're responding to it?

Our obedience is a place of restoration and returning to God. It's a place of glorifying God as we come to our senses and remember his sovereignty. It's a place where our prayers thrive as we continually ask God for guidance and follow-through.

Priscilla Shirer was right. Obedience isn't just some add-on to prayer. It's vital. And if we want to cut through the distance we feel from God, we must decide before we say "Amen" that we won't let emotions dictate our response but that God's will *will* be done in our lives.

When we throw off the weight of emotions and respond to God in obedience, we not only strengthen our ability to hear where God leads in the future but also experience his best-laid plans for our lives.

reflect

What has God told you to do that you've second-guessed or brushed away?

What emotions tend to keep you from obedience most (i.e., fear of the unknown, not wanting to experience discomfort, desire for control, jealousy that God may ask you to do something others don't have to deal with)?

In what moments have you chosen to say yes to God's prompting? What happened?

read

- ○ Luke 6:46-49
- ○ James 1:22-25
- ○ Proverbs 29:11
- ○ Galatians 5:16-18
- ○ Psalm 119, particularly verses 57-61

6

You Loved That Whiner David?

Learning to Lament, Doubt, and Cry Out to God

I AM A GREAT COMPLAINER. You can ask my husband or my sister, and you can most *definitely* ask my mom. I know how to take things that are not at all pointed in my direction, bend them like a spoon with my mind, and make them about me. But complain to God? I would never! Why would I? How could I? How tacky! How classless! How . . . much like, David, the man after God's own heart (see 1 Samuel 13:14).

In the Psalms, we get an inside look into the prayers of David, and it's not what we might expect from a man after God's own heart. We see lots of lamenting and "Why, God?" passages.

One of the hardest ideas for me to grasp about prayer is that God wants me to come to him with every complaint, doubt, or lament. Are we sure God wants to hear this? Didn't the Israelites get in trouble for grumbling and complaining?

Yep. God saved them from slavery in Egypt and helped them cross the Red Sea and get away from the Egyptian army, but the Israelites seemed to forget all of that as soon as their stomachs started growling. In Exodus 16:2-3, we read: "And the whole congregation of the people of Israel grumbled against Moses and Aaron in the wilderness, and the people of Israel said to them, 'Would that we had died by the hand of the LORD in the land of Egypt, when we sat by the meat pots and ate bread to the full, for you have brought us out into this wilderness to kill this whole assembly with hunger.'" Later in the chapter, Moses responds, "When the LORD gives you in the evening meat to eat and in the morning bread to the full, because the LORD has heard your grumbling that you grumble against him—what are we? Your grumbling is not against us but against the LORD" (verse 8).

The problem wasn't *what* the Israelites felt as much as *who* they directed the complaints to. The complaints were not about Moses. They were about God and his provision for them, yet they weren't directed to God. In addition, these weren't just complaints about the way things had turned out. They were huge assumptions about God and his faithfulness to them. This was a long way from honestly bringing their concerns to the Lord.

Somewhere along the way, we got the impression that we need to clean ourselves up before we come to God. We're sure that he doesn't want to see our doubts or hear us complain. And while it's true that God longs to see us have full faith in him and gratitude for everything we've been given, it doesn't mean the answer is to attempt to hide anything from God. Of course nothing is actually hidden from him, but attempting to seal off the closet of complaints from his sight will negatively impact our own hearts.

This is the weight of facades.

We miss out on intimacy and knowing we are fully known and loved by God when we make it look like we have it all together.

Before I met my husband, I remember trying to fathom having someone know all my quirks. You know, like that weird habit you have when you eat. The odd thing you do in your sleep. Or that dumb show you're obsessed with. It felt strange to picture being so incredibly known. Up until that point, it was easy for me to show the very best sides of myself to everyone outside of my family. I didn't even need social media to have a highlight reel. I just put my best foot forward and knew what skeletons to tuck away in the closet.

The thing is, when someone sees all your quirks and bad habits and sticks with you, it deepens the intimacy because you know how fully loved you are. Ten years into marriage, I know I'm not going to scare Tyler off with the real me because he sees it every day. We've already committed to unconditional love, and we didn't base that decision on the assumption that we'd both be perfect and never annoy each other. The idea that I could accidentally show Tyler too much tomorrow doesn't even compute.

> How can we develop intimacy with God if we're always withholding the parts we think he won't like?

Now let's put this in perspective with our prayer lives.

God loves us unconditionally, but how can we fully enjoy his unconditional love if we think it has conditions, like never uttering a complaint or only showing our good sides? How can we develop intimacy with God if we're always withholding the parts we think he won't like?

We simply can't.

And the solution isn't going to be that we should never have doubts or things to complain about. We just have to decide what to do with these thoughts before they even come—and how to bring them to God honestly.

Why We Complain

I cannot tell you the number of times Tyler and I have told our girls, "We're going to [insert place we know they'll like]!" and they've responded with panic or complaints, having no idea what good things were in store. We were patient because we knew they didn't understand. We may have even sat there anticipating the moment when they'd fully understand what we were about to enjoy and they'd change their minds.

God formed our minds. He's well aware of how much we know as well as what we don't know. That unknown is sure to lead to all sorts of questions and even some complaints that come from not fully understanding. This doesn't shock God. I think he responds with patience, much as we do with our kids, knowing that their understanding is limited.

If I can simplify the main reason we complain, here it is: *We complain because we don't see the full picture.* If we did see everything, I think we'd agree with God's plan, but instead, we see just a snippet. We ache as we feel the pain in our own lives, lives that feel like all we have because we can't imagine how they fit into the larger picture of eternity.

Remember when you were young and each birthday felt monumental? You could tell someone how old you were before they finished asking the question. When adults told me they couldn't remember how old they were, I thought my brain must be way better than theirs because that would *never* happen to me. Today's my husband's birthday, and just this morning I had to do the math. *Is he only thirty-five? Wait, no. I think I've been saying he's thirty-five for months now. I just turned thirty-six, and I'm a year older. Or is it just two weeks? Okay, he was born in 1985 and it's 2020, so 2020 minus 1985 is . . . Yep! He's thirty-five! . . . I'm pretty sure.*

The more time we experience or the more years we stack on one another, the easier it is to forget the details. Things that once felt enormous shrink as the span of our life grows. Imagine God, who is outside of time, trying to get us humans, who know only an eighty-year life span, to understand the hope we have in hard seasons. We cannot fathom it because we can't see beyond what's happening in our lives right now. And because we're stuck here, we hurt. We complain.

So how do we make sure the moments of grief and doubt resemble David's lament and not the Israelites' complaining? Here are four essentials that lead to healthy, God-honoring lament.

1. Go Directly to God

We've already said it, but *who* we take our complaint to matters. You might feel like you've got things under control. God's got so much going on, and you hate to be a bother. Surely a complaint about that beach trip you saved up for all year that starts tomorrow and now has an 80 percent chance of thunderstorms the entire week is a first-world problem. (Okay, that was me this week, and it wasn't thunderstorms. It was a hurricane. You read about that earlier.)

I wouldn't think to vent to God about something like this when people are starving around the world, natural disasters are all over the news, and social unrest is at an all-time high. Absolutely not! I would, however, feel perfectly comfortable complaining to my mom and sister. And then complaining some more when we find out last-minute that the lazy river by our rental condo will be under construction and there will be men on our balcony repairing things.

God knows that any hope of transforming our complaints and whines into heart-changing laments is going to come in his presence.

I'll protect God from all my nonsense. It's just feels too petty for God.

This is me completely missing the point of lament prayers. And while I cannot stress enough that this is very much a first-world problem, it's still something I need to take to God. Why? Because my complaints don't stay neatly tucked away in my soul. They fester. They affect my faith. They manifest and move outward, changing my conversations with others. And all this because I feel like it's inappropriate to let God know I have frustrations or doubts. It's faulty logic when I think about it. I can't hide my feelings from him, but for some reason, I think I can still control what God sees of me.

Before we get too far into this topic, I need to clarify something: God doesn't love complaints. God doesn't love whining and ungratefulness. He's not waiting with popcorn to hear us spill the tea about what's bothering us today. He's waiting to change our hearts. God knows that any hope of transforming our complaints and whines into heart-changing laments is going to come in his presence. If we want gratitude and faith to replace the entitlement or doubts in our hearts, it will only happen when we take these things to the one who created those hearts.

When I bring my hurts to God, I'm not lodging them with some faceless department employee who takes down my name to appease me. I'm bringing my issues to the person who cares to fix them and *can* fix them. Not just my situation. In fact, rarely does the answer involve fixing my situation; more often, it involves fixing my heart.

Lamenting to God shows that you know he's the one who can do something with your concerns. Hebrews 4:15-16 says, "For we do not have a high priest who is unable to sympathize with our weaknesses, but one who in every respect has been tempted as we are, yet without sin. Let us then with confidence draw near to the throne of grace, that we may receive mercy and find grace to help in time of need." As I sent ragey text messages to my mom and sister about my vacation problems, I realized I was assuming they could somehow solve this. Voicing those frustrations to my mom and sister revealed who I thought could help.

When you go to God with your frustrations, it's the same thing. And that's actually kind of beautiful. We aren't hopping on the phone with three different friends to vent in order to make ourselves feel better. We're taking our concerns straight to the one who's in control, and we're opening ourselves up to being changed by him.

2. Acknowledge Your Pain

David gets brutally honest with God in many of the psalms. Here's a sampling:

My sighing is not hidden from you.
PSALM 38:9

That's not too bad.

Awake! Why are you sleeping, O Lord?
  Rouse yourself! Do not reject us forever!
Why do you hide your face?
  Why do you forget our affliction and oppression?
For our soul is bowed down to the dust;
  our belly clings to the ground.
Rise up; come to our help!
  Redeem us for the sake of your steadfast love!
PSALM 44:23-26

This is getting uncomfortable.

I am weary with my moaning;
  every night I flood my bed with tears;
  I drench my couch with my weeping.
My eye wastes away because of grief;
  it grows weak because of all my foes.
PSALM 6:6-7

What? "Drench my couch with my weeping"?
These words come from a man full of faith who shared a deep intimacy with the Lord. He still sighed. He still sulked. He still wept and grieved. He felt every emotion and didn't discount any of them. He didn't stuff down his complaints so they could burst forth in a less appropriate way one day.

Ironically, it's the lowest points of our lives that force us

The cries of a lamenter

Psalm 13

1 How long, O LORD? Will you forget me forever?
　How long will you hide your face from me?
2 How long must I take counsel in my soul
　and have sorrow in my heart all the day?
How long shall my enemy be exalted over me?

3 Consider and answer me, O LORD my God;
　light up my eyes, lest I sleep the sleep of death,
4 lest my enemy say, "I have prevailed over him,"
　lest my foes rejoice because I am shaken.

5 But I have trusted in your steadfast love;
　my heart shall rejoice in your salvation.
6 I will sing to the LORD,
　because he has dealt bountifully with me.

[1] Talking directly to the Lord.

[1-2] Acknowledging the complaint. He's torn up and feeling forsaken.

[3-4] David makes his requests. We want answers.

[5-6] Coming back to truth and praise.

---

to get on our knees. When we hit rock bottom, we find ourselves in the prime spot to pray. Honest prayers are birthed in the hard places where we have no more dignity to protect and can't hide the mess we're in. It's like when a child does her best to hide a messy room by barring the doorway with her lanky sixty-pound body. She can't hide a thing, and it's too obvious for her to even pretend she can. So the facades come off. The filter is gone. We stop "behaving" well, hoping for a favorable response. We're finally being authentic.

You might be wrestling with lots of doubts at the moment. Maybe there's sin you keep buried in the closet and have yet to confess. Or perhaps you're grieving and angry at God. Prayer may feel impossible, but you're in a better spot than you think. You have nothing to offer, but that's always been true. It's just more visible now.

Get real with the Lord as David did. He let it all out in the healthiest way possible. Until we do this, we'll create a block between us and God. Our prayers take an unintentionally phony tone when we leave out the giant gaping wound we're carrying.

God can handle the details.

If you're worried about offending God, remember that he is the most sympathetic being in the universe. We're trained to believe that we can offend God just as we can offend another human being. But God is no snowflake. He will not be mocked, but coming humbly to the Lord with hurts and doubts is not mockery. It's honesty.

3. Make Your Request

While David might be one of the most well-known lamenters of the Bible, Joshua had an inspiring lament story too. God had been leading his people into the Promised Land, going before them and helping them defeat the Canaanites. But when the Israelites were routed in battle at the city of Ai, the people were filled with fear.

> And Joshua said, "Alas, O Lord GOD, why have you
> brought this people over the Jordan at all, to give
> us into the hands of the Amorites, to destroy us?
> Would that we had been content to dwell beyond
> the Jordan! O Lord, what can I say, when Israel
> has turned their backs before their enemies! For
> the Canaanites and all the inhabitants of the land
> will hear of it and will surround us and cut off our

name from the earth. And what will you do for
your great name?"
JOSHUA 7:7-9

Joshua was open about his confusion and anguish. Why
was God abandoning his people now? But then God told
him there was more to the story.

> The LORD said to Joshua, "Get up! Why have you
> fallen on your face? Israel has sinned; they have
> transgressed my covenant that I commanded them;
> they have taken some of the devoted things; they
> have stolen and lied and put them among their own
> belongings. Therefore the people of Israel cannot
> stand before their enemies. They turn their backs
> before their enemies, because they have become
> devoted for destruction. I will be with you no
> more, unless you destroy the devoted things from
> among you. Get up! Consecrate the people and say,
> 'Consecrate yourselves for tomorrow; for thus says
> the LORD, God of Israel, "There are devoted things
> in your midst, O Israel. You cannot stand before
> your enemies until you take away the devoted things
> from among you."
> JOSHUA 7:10-13

I can't help but wonder what would have happened if
Joshua had gone to the other leaders and said, "Why is God
doing this? I don't get it. What do we do now?" They might
have all shared in his fear and confusion, but no one would
have had the answer.

Make your requests known to God, and listen for his answer. Don't assume that if he wanted to give you relief, blessing, or freedom from the struggle, he would have already done it. Our God gives good gifts to his children, as we've seen in Matthew 7:11, but he also tells us to ask for them.

Do you have doubts? Give them to him. Tell him. God's not trying to hide truth from you that's necessary for your faith to grow. He longs for you to know him. Ask him to help you see him.

If Joshua hadn't lamented to God, he might have never known the problem. Instead, after the people dealt with it and returned to following God's ways, God helped them return to Ai in victory. What if Joshua had been afraid of sounding upset to God or had assumed he should figure this out on his own? How different could this situation have looked? I have no doubt that God's plans are sovereign and he would still have found a way for the Israelites to return to him and take the land. But how cool that Joshua got to hear directly from God!

I wonder what we miss out on when we're so afraid to ask God something that involves our tears and lament.

4. Praise Well

When we complain to anyone besides God, our experience is hopeless and defeated. But when we lament *to* God, we get out of our personal reality and get into God's. We remind ourselves of the truth and the hope we have in Jesus. This is why praise is a necessary part of lament.

When I come to God about a problem in my heart, I'm saying, "I don't want to feel this way, but this is the reality. I don't want to have so much pride that I try to hide this from you. I know you're good, you're powerful, and you know best. I praise you because you're the best thing in my life no matter what is happening."

Again, I don't think God tells us to come to him with all our drama and lament because he loves it but because he loves *us*. He rightly knows he's the one who can redeem all our complaints and comfort us in our laments. He loves our being real. He loves what happens when we stop putting up a wall of pretense and instead fall in his arms because we're no longer hiding our real selves.

Selah.

We won't find the hope of Jesus while we're licking our wounds in a corner by ourselves.

I want to say praise is the final destination, but much like David in Psalm 13 and many other psalms, we'll seesaw back and forth from lament to praise. We'll need to keep reminding ourselves of truth. In those psalm verses, when David talks about the fact that he can trust God, I don't think he quickly got over his tears. I don't think he was suddenly good with his problems. It's like he was reminding himself of the truth—the things he knew in his mind but had to remind his heart of.

We need to remember that lament is a messy process. Just because we fall back into doubt or laments or grief or tears doesn't mean things are hopeless.

One day, as I was driving on the interstate, grieving the loss of an opportunity for our business, I burst into tears. Lyrics came to mind, and I sang them through tears of sadness:

All my life You have been faithful
All my life You have been so, so good.[1]

I knew those words were true, but I still hurt. I still felt sadness, but I also felt hope in the truth about God that remained no matter what I was facing in the moment.

You have that hope too. Don't be afraid of your hurts and doubts. Don't be afraid of your frustrations with God. Take them to him. That's the most important part to remember. Our doubts must not cause us to neglect prayer. If they do, we'll experience a weight in our prayer lives that God never asked us to carry. Release that weight and grab hold instead of the God who loves us so unconditionally that David, the notoriously dramatic pray-er, could be called the man after God's own heart and could experience such intimacy with God. When we throw off the weight of facades and come to God with our complaints and laments, we realize we are fully known and loved by God.

reflect

Can you think of anything you need to grieve over in the presence of the Lord?

What does it look like to release your complaints to him so they don't fester?

When you're in the midst of suffering, what truth do you need to recall about eternity that would expand the praise you offer?

read

○ Psalm 102:1-2
○ Matthew 11:28-30
○ Psalm 130
○ Psalm 142:1-2

7

How about We Go with My Plan?

Giving Up Control and Trusting God's Will

IN HIGH SCHOOL, I prayed something that was far more audacious and risky than I realized in the moment. I'd read a book about marriage by Elisabeth Elliot, and she said that while she was single, she'd asked God to put her desires to sleep like God put Adam to sleep before he created Eve—and then to reawaken them only in his timing. I decided that was a pretty good prayer. I longed to keep my heart and body pure for marriage and thought this would save me lots of heartache and mistakes.

It may have kept me from some mistakes, but it didn't save me from all heartache. I spent the first twenty-four years of my life (minus a week in sixth grade and another week in college) utterly and completely single. From the time I was old enough to date, it was a series of "I like him, but he doesn't like me" or "He likes me, but I don't like him" moments.

I remember regretting that prayer. Couldn't I just have one good date? One rom-com moment? One exciting kiss?

I have journals and journals filled with prayers like *God, have you forgotten about me?* or *Why do my roommates have so many boyfriends and I can't scare one up?** I wish I could explain how much time I spent thinking God had gotten something wrong or obviously didn't care about me.

But then, after nearly twenty-four years of straight singleness, I fell in love with the guy who was right under my nose, my best friend and co-owner of our short-lived joint stationery venture, Butterscotch Press. When I finally realized I'd be Mrs. Woerner one day soon, I wrote something in my journal even more audacious than that first prayer: "Well, that didn't take too long."

I wasn't being sarcastic. Suddenly it felt like the years had rushed by. I couldn't believe how perfect God's timing was and how quickly he had brought Tyler into my life. In a moment, I switched gears from wishing I had more control of the plan to being grateful God hadn't been weak enough to be manipulated into giving in after my years of whining.

It was easy to trust God when I got to see his plan finally unfold, but I wish I had trusted him more in the seasons where I thought my plan was better because, frankly, it didn't look like God had a plan at all.

This is the weight of control.

We miss out on blessing along the journey when we want to go our own way instead of trusting in God.

The weight of control looks like spending our precious prayer time asking for things that don't align with God's will

---

*Okay, it wasn't that many. My memory that each of my three roommates had dates every night of the weekend may be slightly exaggerated. But isn't that how we feel when we're not in control? Like everyone's grass is greener than ours?

at all—and then, when they don't happen, suddenly blaming him for not loving us or not being powerful enough to handle our problems.

Maybe you've prayed for success in business because you desperately want to be seen by others. Or maybe you've prayed for a skinny body because you don't believe you can be comfortable in your skin at your current weight. Maybe you've prayed for life to stop handing you trials without knowing that those trials are transforming you into the person who's going to handle the next season with grace and joy.

Our prayer lives will remain stuck if we continue to seek our own will over God's. We'll get no after no and start to wonder if praying is worth it. That reaction won't bring us into thriving prayer lives with our Father. He wants our hearts, and he wants us to come to him with our every desire. That's where he transforms us: in his presence.

> **Our prayer lives will remain stuck if we continue to seek our own will over God's.**

Assuming "God's just going to do what he wants anyway" is the equivalent of taking our ball and going home. We opt out. Control, on the other hand, is trying to wrestle the ball out of God's hands so we can play by our own rules. We come to prayer with the wrong agenda.

What's the alternative? Gently coming under the wing of God's sovereignty with *everything* we have because we understand that his mission is our mission too.

God's Plan Won't Be Steamrolled

One of my new favorite unexpected prayer lessons in the Bible is when Jesus turned water into wine. When Jesus, the disciples, and Jesus' mom, Mary, attended a wedding and the hosts ran out of wine—an embarrassing situation in that culture—Mary asked Jesus to help.

In John 2:4, Jesus replied, "Woman, what does this have to do with me? My hour has not yet come." Surprisingly, his mother's response to this statement was to tell the servants, "Do whatever he tells you" (verse 5). Following his instructions, they filled several big stone jars with water, then drew some out and brought it to the master of the feast. When he tasted it, it had become wine.

I always wondered a few things about this story. First, did Mary steamroll Jesus with her response? She knew he was the Son of God, and I have to imagine she'd noticed he somehow remained holy through the toddler years. Why didn't she trust his timing here? Also, why did Jesus do the miracle if he knew his time hadn't come?

This shouldn't surprise you, but I don't have all the answers. What I do know after reading the passage a little more slowly is this: Jesus perfectly managed the tension of performing the miracle while not contradicting what he'd just said. The water was turned to wine, but verse 9 says the master "did not know where [the wine] came from." Jesus was able to respond to his mom's requests without forsaking God's will and the timing of when his "hour" would come.

Mission accomplished.

Mary's comment wasn't an actual prayer, but I think it's a pretty spot-on example of what it looks like to pray to God. We aren't twisting his arm, and we'll never get God to go against his will, but within his plan, there's some wiggle room.*

Jesus successfully blessed the wedding, his mom, and the

---

*I'm not talking about all roads or religions leading to heaven. There's no wiggle room in the path to God. Jesus is "the way, and the truth, and the life. No one comes to the Father except through" him (John 14:6). But R. C. Sproul says, "There is freedom within limits, and within those limits, our prayers can change things."[1]

guests when he turned water into wine, all while not making a big public display of his power or going against God's plan. Verse 11 continues, "This, the first of his signs, Jesus did at Cana in Galilee, and manifested his glory. And his disciples believed in him."

The result of this miracle was that the disciples believed. I have no idea what different circumstances would have arisen to help the disciples believe if Jesus had not performed this particular miracle. All I know is that God used it to the fullest, and he got the glory.

I believe God changes things because of the prayers of his kids. Not because we came up with a better idea than his but because he can do generous and loving things *within his will*.

This idea that our prayers can change our circumstances can make believers feel uncomfortable. How can this be true? Are we more powerful than God? Are we calling the shots? Is he that impressionable?

The short answer? We can't control God.

God's love and generosity work in tandem with his unchanging nature. God will not go against his character to answer our prayers—and that just might be the most generous and loving thing he can do for us. Can you even imagine if God said yes to our every request?

It makes me reexamine Matthew 7, where Jesus tells us to ask of God and then says, "Which one of you, if his son asks him for bread, will give him a stone? . . . If you then, who are evil, know how to give good gifts to your children, how much more will your Father who is in heaven give good things to those who ask him!" (verses 9, 11). We know God is good and loving, so maybe those unanswered prayers we see as unloving are just an example of God not giving us a stone.

Our perceptions are affected by the world (see James 4:2-4). The world will convince us a stone tastes delicious. It may work overtime to make us believe that a God who *won't* give us that stone is mean and obviously doesn't care for us. It sounds comical, but it's actually quite easy to think this way when we are so closely entangled with the world.

But God will not be steamrolled. So when we're affected by the world and we pray for things that actually aren't beneficial, he will say no. And that's his mercy at work because it means we can ask boldly and then humbly trust that he will do what is best. He invites us to ask, and sometimes he changes things because of our prayers, but he won't let us thwart his good plans.

God's Purpose Is Bigger Than We Can See

Each of the four Gospels covers Jesus' life with a different purpose. Matthew is written to show Jesus as the long-awaited king; Mark shows Jesus as servant; Luke shows Jesus as man. John's purpose is for us to know Jesus is the divine Son of God.[2] He stays on theme so well that we're going to hit a few more passages in his Gospel. Several repeated phrases are "believe," "signs," and "so that you may believe." At the end of the book, in John 20:31, he pulls it all together: "These are written so that you may believe that Jesus is the Christ, the Son of God, and that by believing you may have life in his name."

As we address how our desire for control can weigh us down in prayer, I think it's vital we really understand how our stories intersect with God's greater purpose.

John 11 contains the story of Jesus raising Lazarus from the dead. It's a stark reminder that our timing is not God's timing. Lazarus's sisters, Mary and Martha, try to reach Jesus when their brother is sick and dying. But instead of hurrying to their side, as we'd expect Jesus to do, he waits a few days. And by the time he arrives, Lazarus is already dead.

Jesus is too late.

No.

Actually, Jesus is never too late. What looks late to people is right on time to God. This was true for Lazarus, and it's true for us, too.

Goodness, that's hard for me to wrap my head around when I'm waiting and praying and waiting some more. Have you ever felt like God showed up late

> **Jesus is never too late. What looks late to people is right on time to God.**

in your life? Are you currently sitting around wondering where he is but suspecting his absence must be a mistake? Was it traffic? Did he just get started late this morning? Is he preoccupied with someone else's needs? Did he forget he had a prior engagement when you asked him to show up?

Selah. Hit pause. Lift up your needs in prayer and ask God to speak to you as you keep reading. We're all waiting on something. Voice it to the one who has ultimate control.

I have to imagine Lazarus's sisters felt the same disappointment and even betrayal we can feel in the unclear moments. Here's one reason I love this story, though: The purpose is so clear. There's no doubt that God's timing was just as he planned because we get to hear the reasons for Jesus' delay over and over in the passage.

> But when Jesus heard it he said, "This illness does
> not lead to death. It is *for the glory of God,* so that the
> *Son of God may be glorified through it.*"
> VERSE 4, EMPHASIS ADDED

> Then Jesus told them plainly, "Lazarus has died, and
> for your sake I am glad that I was not there, so *that
> you may believe*. But let us go to him."
> VERSES 14-15, EMPHASIS ADDED

> Jesus said to her, "Did I not tell you that if *you
> believed you would see the glory of God*?"
> VERSE 40, EMPHASIS ADDED

> Many of the Jews therefore, who had come with
> Mary and had seen what he did, *believed in him*.
> VERSE 45, EMPHASIS ADDED

And guess what? Even those who opposed Jesus caught on to God's purpose! In John 11:47-48, the chief priests and Pharisees reacted to the news of Lazarus's resurrection by saying, "For this man [Jesus] performs many signs. If we let him go on like this, everyone will believe in him." The seemingly late arrival of Jesus meant the faith of many.

Our greatest commission here on earth is to point others to God. Creation does it, and we're called to do it too. Everything is for the glory of God. The "late" arrival of Jesus in your life and the future answered prayer may mean someone else will discover the living God.

What the priests and Pharisees feared happening is the outcome *we* pursue—that people would know and believe God. If the result of miracles and answered prayers is that others will know and believe, let us not give up praying for what we're waiting on and let us absolutely give God the glory when things happen. No matter how late the answers appear, our prayers are part of a bigger story. And I often see this more clearly in the Bible than I can in my own life.

You see, just prior to Lazarus being resurrected, Jesus was confronted at the Feast of Dedication when he said that he and the Father were one (see John 10:22-38). The religious leaders, of course, thought this was blasphemy and wanted to stone him. Right before Jesus commanded Lazarus to come out of the tomb (and be raised), he said these words: "Father, I thank you that you have heard me. I knew that you always hear me, but I said this on account of the people standing around, *that they may believe that you sent me*" (John 11:41-42, emphasis added).

So essentially, on the heels of Jesus saying he and the Father are one, he performed a miracle showing people how true his words were. Mary and Martha likely had no idea of this backstory. They were lamenting a dead brother and were justifiably focused within their own four walls, wondering how a loving God could let their brother die.

As I see the fullness of this story, I'm overwhelmed by the bigger picture that I so easily forget as I plot what I think is the best plan. I'm desperate to have my personal problem fixed today, completely forgetting that the goal of my life on earth is not for me to be comfortable but for me to go and make disciples.

Tim Keller says, "God will either give us what we ask for in prayer or give us what we would have asked for if we knew everything he knows."[3] If there's one big thing I've learned from the Bible, it's that I pray a lot without knowing everything. In fact, I always pray without knowing everything. So many factors go into the way my prayers are answered, and they don't all have to do with only me. How would our prayers change if we remembered that the loving God who seems to be late has the full picture of humanity in mind, and our momentary pain may mean eternal redemption for someone who is a witness to it?

I'm grateful Jesus didn't only worry about Mary and Martha's temporary tears at the cost of others getting to know the one true God. Yet if I were one of the sisters, I fear I may have been the one to jokingly bump Jesus after he raised Lazarus, saying, "How could you put us through that!" and being completely focused on the temporary roller coaster of emotions.*

I also believe this miracle took place in the life of one of Jesus' own friends so we could see that Jesus felt the emotional roller coaster too. John 11:35 says, "Jesus wept." He felt the pain of the wait when he witnessed his friend dead and others grieving. Yet even knowing he would experience that pain, because he knew God's purpose, he still waited those two days to arrive.

Friends, may we wait with hope in the greater story that is happening. Knowing we're a part of that story doesn't wipe away our tears, just as it didn't take away Jesus' tears, but it gives us endurance to wait with hope. And it prompts us to keep letting go of control because we know that God's answer will always be better than the one we came up with.

God Is Generous with Context Clues

Let's continue through John, shall we? One of the most misunderstood verses on prayer shows up in John 14:13: "Whatever you ask in my name, this I will do, that the Father may be glorified in the Son."

As I read John in its entirety, I see what drives Jesus to make such an audacious promise. Maybe he assumed we

---

*Right here is where I remind us that not all stories end with a raising of the dead. We might go to our graves not seeing the rest of the story, but the good news is that our stories don't end with the grave.

heard the whole message and didn't just wake up for what we'd call the climax of the story. Here's what I see Jesus saying in the book of John:

> Yet I do not seek my own glory; there is One who seeks it, and he is the judge.
> JOHN 8:50

> We know that God does not listen to sinners, but if anyone is a worshiper of God and does his will, God listens to him.
> JOHN 9:31

> My sheep hear my voice, and I know them, and they follow me.
> JOHN 10:27

> Whoever loves his life loses it, and whoever hates his life in this world will keep it for eternal life.
> JOHN 12:25

> For they loved the glory that comes from man more than the glory that comes from God.
> JOHN 12:43

These words come from the one who also said to ask whatever you wish. This is important context. He makes these things clear: Followers of God actually follow him. They live for eternal things. They love the glory that comes from God and not people. There's a pattern emerging, highlighting that followers of Jesus aren't motivated by selfishness or our own comfort. We're called to be God centered.

When we're weighed down by the desire to control outcomes and get what we want, how often do we ask for things that contradict a God-centered mission? When we pray, is our focus that God will look good and that his name will be honored?

God Wants Us to Pray According to His Will

John's not done yet.

In chapter 15, he shares Jesus' teaching of the vine: "If you abide in me, and my words abide in you, ask whatever you wish, and it will be done for you. By this my Father is glorified, that you bear much fruit and so prove to be my disciples" (verses 7-8).

I know you didn't buy this book just to read Scripture I copied and pasted in it, but I don't want us to miss this. Prayer can feel mysterious, almost as if God doesn't want us to understand it. *Why make it so hard if you want us to talk to you, God?* Yet as I read Scripture on the hunt for everything related to prayer, my mind is blown by how clear it is. Four times within the span of just a few chapters, Jesus tells us to ask whatever we wish in his Father's name. He's starting to sound like a broken record, but themes are repeated for a purpose. I think this repetition is a reminder that God has an *unbroken* record. He didn't lie. He's promised us the same thing four times and it's true. We just sometimes let our own hang-ups convince us otherwise.

In the last of the four instances (John 16:23-24), Jesus drops the hammer: "Truly, truly, I say to you, whatever you ask of the Father in my name, he will give it to you. Until now you have asked nothing in my name. Ask, and you will receive, that your joy may be full."

We don't have because we aren't asking in his name!

"In my name" can be confusing, but I love how Eugene Peterson paraphrases it in *The Message*: "Whatever you request *along the lines of who I am and what I am doing*, I'll do it" (John 14:13, emphasis added). I love that. "Along the lines of *who I am* and *what I am doing*."

Does this factor into my prayers? When I try to control the outcome, am I praying along the lines of who Jesus is and what he is doing? How do I even know what these things are?

This passage suggests that when it seems like God isn't answering, it's because we're either not asking at all or we're not asking in God's name. Perhaps instead we're asking in *our* name. And God never promised that we would have whatever we ask in our own names. What amazing things are we missing out on because we're praying for the trial to go away instead of asking God to give us peace as we walk through it? He's promised to bring us peace when we stay fixed on him (see Isaiah 26:3). That's part of who he is and what he's doing. He hasn't promised that the trial will go away.

I understand that this can get dicey. We can swing in the other direction completely and fear praying anything without tagging it with a closing signature: "If it's your will, Lord." But I believe the deeper we know God, the more freedom we will feel from these fears. We will hear his whisper. We will sense his nudge. We won't aimlessly be praying . . . *but if not, that's cool too, God. Whatever you want is fine.*

When we know God, we can pray with conviction. When we know Scripture, we can confidently ask because we know what aligns with God's mission—maybe not the minute details but the overall picture.

tip

Here are some promises that can anchor your prayers. Ask the Lord to give you an understanding of what these promises truly mean. A promise that God supplies our needs or calms our fears can cause us doubt if we've prayed and then faced hardship or continued to walk in fear. But when we believe God's Word, we trust that these promises are true and ask God to show us how he is working them out in our lives.

- **God will guide us.** "Trust in the LORD with all your heart and lean not on your own understanding; in all your ways submit to him, and he will make your paths straight" (Proverbs 3:5-6, NIV).
- **God will be with us through hard times.** "When you pass through the waters, I will be with you; and when you pass through the rivers, they will not sweep over you. When you walk through the fire, you will not be burned; the flames will not set you ablaze" (Isaiah 43:2, NIV).
- **God listens to those who call on him.** "Then you will call on me and come and pray to me, and I will listen to you" (Jeremiah 29:12, NIV).
- **God gives rest to those who come to him.** "Come to me, all you who are weary and burdened, and I will give you rest. Take my yoke upon you and learn from me, for I am gentle and humble in heart, and you will find rest for your souls. For my yoke is easy and my burden is light" (Matthew 11:28-30, NIV).
- **God produces fruit in those who abide in him.** "Yes, I am the vine; you are the branches. Those who remain in me, and I in them, will produce much fruit. For apart from me you can do nothing" (John 15:5, NLT).
- **God gives wisdom to those who ask.** "If any of you lacks wisdom, you should ask God, who gives generously to all without finding fault, and it will be given to you" (James 1:5, NIV).
- **God promises salvation to those that confess Jesus as Lord.** "If you confess with your mouth that Jesus is Lord and believe in your heart that God raised him from the dead, you will be saved" (Romans 10:9).

What if we started understanding who Jesus is and what he is doing, as Eugene Peterson mentioned? What if we made prayer less about us and more about him?

In John 17, we get to hear one of Jesus' own prayers before his arrest. It's long, but I challenge you to read the whole thing because hearing the very prayers of Jesus is such a beautiful way to learn to pray! One thing jumps out at me. Even in this worst of times, right before his betrayal and death, Jesus was *still* determined to give God glory. His prayer is peppered with phrases such as the following:

- "Glorify your Son that the Son may glorify you" (verse 1).
- "I glorified you on earth, having accomplished the work that you gave me to do" (verse 4).
- "I have manifested your name to the people" (verse 6).
- "They know that everything that you have given me is from you" (verse 7).

If glorifying God were my mission too, it would naturally shift my prayers. What might our prayers sound like if they really echoed the heart of God and if we were so about our Father's business? I bet the weight would fall right off as we simply changed our trajectory to point directly to God. When we throw off the weight of control and seek God's glory rather than our own comfort, we gain the blessings of being part of a grander story that's bigger than we ever dreamed.

reflect

What cliché things are you praying for or demanding from God that he never actually promised?

What has God promised us? Make a list and keep it handy as you pray.

Take a minute to consider: Are you pursuing God's will as you pray or just wanting to address your personal agenda?

read

- ○ Jeremiah 32:27
- ○ Psalm 33:8-11
- ○ Proverbs 3:5-6
- ○ Joshua 1:9

throwing off the weights that keep us
from fully entering the conversation

8

Where Did You Go, God?

Drawing Near to God in the Valley

I REMEMBER WHEN my relationship with the Lord started
to take shape. I was in the high school youth group at my
church, and a small group of girls had just gone through
a study that taught us what it looked like to spend quality
time with the Lord. I began to not only make time to pray or
read my Bible in the mornings but actually desire it too. My
relationship with God was finally my own. When you grow
up in a Christian home where you've been doing all the same
things simply because that's how it's done, this simple light
bulb in your own heart can be huge.

Soon after, I got interested in a blue-haired boy we'll
call Bob.* He wasn't a believer, but since he was attending a
Christian school, I made the assumption he was and fell hard

---

*I should clarify that he had dyed his hair cotton-candy blue—just in case you thought I was using "blue"
the way some refer to gray hair. No, he was not an elderly man, just a rebel teen who didn't want to fit in.

for him. By the time he expressed his beliefs, or lack thereof, and I realized we weren't on the same page faith-wise, I tried to justify up and down why it was okay for us to date. I might also clarify right here that boys were *not* beating down my door. When we really want something, it's easy to convince ourselves that the wrong choice is still better than nothing.

I remember standing on the curb at Bob's house before I headed to a week of camp in Colorado with my church youth group. I told him I felt God would tell me on that trip whether we should be dating. Looking back, I wonder what Bob must have thought of me. *I believe in God. You don't believe in God. I'm going to ask God what he thinks I should do about dating you.* He was gracious as I told him we'd talk when I got back from the mountains with God's answer.

The audacity I had. I'm still not sure why I was so confident, other than that the Lord gave me the confidence.

As we approached the camp, my sensitive ears felt so much pain.* One night, as I was tucked in my sleeping bag, my ears and fears rattled, I grabbed my flashlight and flipped to a random page in my devotional. I remember these words: *Marrying an unbeliever is like being shackled. Don't do it (see 2 Corinthians 6:14).*

In that moment, I knew beyond a shadow of a doubt that the Lord was real. I knew he heard me, and I knew he cared about me. This was no coincidence. This was the clarity I'd hoped God would give me. I wasn't thinking about marriage yet, of course, but I was reminded that dating is the first step. That moment, knowing that God could so faithfully answer me, was a turning point in my young faith and an incredible

---

*To get technical, I have small Eustachian tubes and had already experienced two burst eardrums due to elevation and pressure changes. Even a slow climb in the mountains by church van was excruciating.

boost to my prayer life. I wished the answer had been different, but I was way more captivated by a God who became personal to me than by that blue-haired boy.

What I would have given to hear the Lord so clearly in 2016.

The year started off with a girl (that'd be me) desperately praying but feeling like my words bounced right off the ceiling and knocked me to the floor. I've never felt so discouraged in my prayer life as in that season. Deep down, I knew God was at work, but the evidence before me made it nearly impossible to see. I'm not sure what prompted the loss of hope, but it didn't let up. Then Tyler and I saw unexpected death in my extended family, walked through terminal cancer with a loved one, survived a flood, and experienced business struggles all in the span of four months.

When we face moments like these, we often pull back because it sure feels like God pulled back first. How could he let all this happen? Why does it feel like every prayer is going straight to voicemail? Why stick around if he's already peaced out and we have no way of knowing when he'll come back?

Why pray when God feels so far away?

This is the weight of distance.

We miss out on God's comfort in the hard times when we move away from him because we hoped for something different.

I think there are four ways we experience distance from the Lord, and each requires a different primary response. When we're fleeing from God and choosing other loves, we need to fight the distractions, repent, and pursue him. When we're wandering through a wilderness of testing, we need to rest in the work God is doing. When we're idling on an island, we need to praise God in the waiting. And when we're deserted with a no in the desert, we need to trust God's plans.

Fleeing through the Forest (Choice)

The first way we feel distance from God is perhaps the one we think of most often: when we *choose* to add distance by our own actions. Those actions can take the form of not confessing sin, harboring unforgiveness, filling our minds with worldly things, and even simply being too busy for God.

Like characters in a fairy tale who get lost in the woods, we're following a trail of distractions and temptations the enemy has laid out for us, each one looking more appetizing than the last and each one sending us deeper into the forest and farther away from God. At a certain point, we see how far away we are, but we still don't turn around to try and find our way back. We choose to keep wandering, to go our own way and follow what looks most appealing rather than what is best.

> **What are the choices I'm making right now that are keeping me from intimacy with God?**

Isaiah 59:1-2 says, "Listen! The Lord's arm is not too weak to save you, nor is his ear too deaf to hear you call. It's your sins that have cut you off from God. Because of your sins, he has turned away and will not listen anymore" (NLT). Isaiah is essentially telling the nation of Israel, "Want to know why you feel distant from God? It's you, not him! God hasn't changed; you have."

We want to blame God when he feels distant, but the choices we make on a daily basis will influence our prayer lives. That may be the simplest sentence I can write in this book, but it's a truth we often forget. I need to ask myself,

What are the choices I'm making right now that are keeping me from intimacy with God?

You might do a heart check and see unconfessed sin or laziness. You might discover that God has called you to do something, and you haven't done it. Pursue God. Fight. Fight by confessing your own part in the distance and then return to the things God has already called every believer to do: pray, meditate on his Word, worship him, and love others well. God doesn't require us to fix the distance between us. He closes the gap, but he tells us to call to him.

I'm actually thankful for the discomfort I feel when I'm distant from the Lord as a result of choosing him less and less. Why? Because if everything felt fine and normal, I'd get further and further into the woods of my own choices. Instead, I notice when I'm not experiencing intimacy with God. I'm selfish with my husband, I'm impatient with my

---

tip ───────────────────────────────

What are some practical ways we can choose God?

1. Pray for an awareness of the things that you may be choosing over intimacy with God. They may be really subtle (James 1:5).
2. Set firm boundaries on the obvious offenders, such as screens. I shouldn't need to wonder why I feel far from God when I spend five minutes in prayer each day but five hours looking at social media (Romans 12:2).
3. Have a friend who keeps you accountable. I think we miss out on the biggest blessing of friendship when we don't allow someone else access to our struggles and rough edges. So much refinement happens when we get close to others (Proverbs 27:17).

---

kids, and everyone offends me. Want more? I feel shame when I should feel grace. I indulge myself when I should show self-control. I withhold when I should be generous. I trudge through reading the Word instead of feeling refreshed by Scripture. I drift off in prayer instead of being captivated by talking to the God of the universe.

When choices create distance between you and God, keep it simple. Choose God.

Wandering in the Wilderness (Testing)

My college had a monthly service called Commonground where all the campus ministries united for a message and a time of worship. One evening, the speaker shared about a dry season in his life, and it was the first time I realized faithful believers who were actively pursuing the Lord could go through dry seasons.

Sometimes we create distance by fleeing. At other times, God creates the distance. I know what you're thinking: *God doesn't move away from me. He's always there.* That doesn't stop being true. But God is at work in our lives to grow our trust in him, and sometimes he allows us to feel distance and deal with circumstances that will mature our faith.

James 1:2-4 says, "Consider it pure joy, my brothers and sisters, whenever you face trials of many kinds, because you know that the testing of your faith produces perseverance. Let perseverance finish its work so that you may be mature and complete, not lacking anything" (NIV). In those moments when you're pursuing God faithfully, examining your heart, confessing sin, and drawing near to God yet still feeling something missing, you may be in a season of testing.

It's not a punishment. It's a place of growth.

And it might be a season we don't anxiously need to claw our way out of. That might sound crazy. Of course we want to feel close to God and experience his presence. If you've ever felt far from God and didn't want to, you know how anxious you feel to return to a "healthy spot." But we forgo the value of the season we're in when we're constantly trying to escape it.

Based on my experience, these are some indicators that we need to sit still—to rest—and embrace the wilderness:

- **You pursue the Lord wholeheartedly and still feel unmoved.** If I'm in a spiritual funk because I've chosen to fill my mind with too much Netflix, putting in extra time in the Word refreshes my soul and bears fruit. Even if it's not huge, the hint of freshness helps me keep connecting with the Lord. But in those moments when I'm faithfully coming to the Lord and still feeling like my prayers hit a ceiling, I know it's time to rest. That doesn't mean I toss my Bible and stop trying to connect with the Lord; I keep on praying and reading. But it means I stop trying to run from a season that I'm obviously in for a reason, and I trust that God has a purpose for it.

- **You can sit in the season without sinking deeper.** Our enemy is planting lies in our minds, and if resting in a season of distance leads to our believing things that go against Scripture, then we're relaxing when we should be battling the enemy. First Peter 5:8-9 says, "Be sober-minded; be watchful. Your adversary the devil prowls around like a roaring lion, seeking someone to devour." If we're getting more depressed, more discouraged, more doubtful of the Lord, then we need to start fighting and have others fight for us too through prayer and active support. But if we can sit in the season with our trust in God intact, then we're right to rest and watch to see how God is at work.

- **You're still filled with hope in a dry season.** Not only are we *not* sinking deeper; we're feeling hope that things will improve. Marriage offers a great example. Spouses need to be intentional about spending time together and investing in their marriage, but we have busy seasons where time is harder to come by. Tyler and I have walked through these seasons where we simply hug each other as we part for the day, knowing the temporary distance isn't destroying us. It's no way to live long-term, but we're confident in what we've built and know that it can sustain a short season of less quality time. When we're in a wilderness season with God, we can feel hopeful because we're certain that our relationship with him is strong enough to last through the testing period and emerge even better than before.

- **You see fruit (see Galatians 5:22-23).** Fruit is a sign of maturity, a reminder that we are still connected to the vine. In John 15:5 Jesus says, "I am the vine; you are the branches. Whoever abides in me and I in him, he it is that bears much fruit, for apart from me you can do nothing." If you are experiencing fruit in a season of distance, be reminded that growing closer to God doesn't always involve a feeling but can be the visible fruit that's sprouting in your life. Maybe your compassion for others increased after you walked through loneliness, or your ability to be content came after a long season of feeling like God didn't provide enough.

In seasons of testing, abide in the vine. Rest in God. Soak up moments with him without being consumed with the desire to feel connection. Ironically, sometimes getting back the loving feeling becomes an idol. Tim Keller says, "A counterfeit god is anything so central and essential to your life that, should you lose it, your life would feel hardly worth living."[1] When we focus on how God makes us feel instead of on God himself, we spin our wheels trying to get back to feeling good with God without realizing he's still with us. I guess that's what I'm trying to articulate when I say we need to rest. Let your growing faith remind you that God is there and he's doing good work in you even if he feels distant.

Idling on an Island (Waiting)

Waiting feels like a curse word among some Christians. We talk about it with such sadness. When someone mentions waiting for God to answer a prayer request or change something in his or her life, we're able to relate because we're waiting on God to do something too. And though people can relate, we can feel isolated, trapped—like we're stuck on an island with no escape.

The rational explanation for our waiting is that God forgot about us. We're so small, and the world is so big. People are starving. Freedoms are stolen. Diagnoses are delivered. Marriages are ending. Whatever we're waiting on, no matter how big, there's always something bigger that can convince us God has his hands too full to help us. Or maybe we think that God just doesn't care about us. If he did, he'd notice how much we're struggling and answer us more quickly.

Our natural response to waiting is often *We'll just catch up when God comes back. I'll go about my daily life and talk to God when I can actually see he's here, but until then, I'll manage on my own.* So many times, we're not even angry as we wait. We're just tired of bringing up the same thing in prayer. Surely, if God wanted to or could do anything, he would have by now. It feels hopeless.

I wonder how hopeless Joseph felt.

Joseph was the kid brother who was sold into slavery by his own older brothers (see Genesis 37). Then he was thrown into prison for something he never did (see Genesis 39). Then he was forgotten in prison after he helped another prisoner get free (see Genesis 40).

Four times in chapter 39, we get a reminder that the Lord was with Joseph. I'm so glad these reminders are there because as we read what Joseph goes through, it's enough to make us assume that God was most definitely not with him.

- Genesis 39:2—"*The LORD was with Joseph,* and he became a successful man, and he was in the house of his Egyptian master" (emphasis added).
- Genesis 39:3—"His master saw that *the LORD was with him* and that the LORD caused all that he did to succeed in his hands" (emphasis added).
- Genesis 39:21—"But *the LORD was with Joseph* and showed him steadfast love and gave him favor in the sight of the keeper of the prison" (emphasis added).
- Genesis 39:23—"The keeper of the prison paid no attention to anything that was in Joseph's charge, because *the LORD was with him.* And whatever he did, the LORD made it succeed" (emphasis added).

Can you imagine if we punctuated the hard moments of life with "and the Lord was with me"? Let's not just imagine.

Let's do it right now. Identify what you are currently waiting for and sprinkle "and the Lord was with me" throughout your description.

- Tony lost his job, and the Lord was with him.
- Laura received a cancer diagnosis, and the Lord was with her.
- One of Sandy's children struggled with substance abuse, and the Lord was with her.
- Shannon was unfairly blamed for a mistake at work, and the Lord was with her.

Selah.

What does that change? It doesn't take away the hurt, but it certainly brings hope in the midst of the wait. We are not forgotten. We might feel like it, but God does not forget. I can't say for sure how forgotten Joseph felt, but at one point, he says, "For I was indeed stolen out of the land of the Hebrews, and here also I have done nothing that they should put me into the pit" (Genesis 40:15). This doesn't sound to me like a man who feels he's right where God called him to be.

A few chapters later, Joseph sees why he was meant to go through all this. He's pulled out of prison to interpret Pharaoh's dream and then ends up being put into a position of power. He can now acknowledge God's hand on his life this whole time. He tells his brothers,

Do not be distressed or angry with yourselves because you sold me here, for God sent me before you to preserve life. For the famine has been in the land these two years, and there are yet five years in which there

will be neither plowing nor harvest. And God sent
me before you to preserve for you a remnant on earth,
and to keep alive for you many survivors. *So it was not
you who sent me here, but God.*
GENESIS 45:5-8, EMPHASIS ADDED

I mentioned earlier that *waiting* feels like a curse word
to Christians. But I'm learning that waiting is good and in-
evitable, not a hard thing we *may* face. Waiting is a necessary
part of the process of living the human life. It doesn't only
happen to those who are forgotten or those who failed. We
should expect periods of waiting. I wonder when we started
feeling so blindsided by it?

This natural part of life is something we can praise God
for. We don't have to know all the details to know it's good
because we already know and trust that our God is good.

Dick Eastman says, "Waiting on the Lord is basically the
silent surrendering of the soul to God."[2] See what Scripture
tells us about waiting:

I will wait for your name, for it is good,
    in the presence of the godly.
PSALM 52:9

My soul waits for the Lord
    more than watchmen for the morning,
    more than watchmen for the morning.
PSALM 130:6

They who wait for the LORD shall renew their strength;
    they shall mount up with wings like eagles.
ISAIAH 40:31

Good stuff happens in the wait. It feels painful and threatens our intimacy with the Lord, but it can also draw us nearer. It's hard *not* to recognize the beauty of that.

Deserted in the Desert ("Nos")

Jesus said to his disciples, "For truly, I say to you, if you have faith like a grain of mustard seed, you will say to this mountain, 'Move from here to there,' and it will move, and nothing will be impossible for you" (Matthew 17:20). So how can we have moments of full faith where the mountains don't move—when we get a flat-out no from God? Feeling deserted when God doesn't answer is the fourth kind of distance we can experience.

I've gotten "nos" before. And I've been able to look back on most of those times and see that God was clearly right.

God's "No, I won't make you popular in high school" led to "Thank you, God, for keeping me away from too many parties where I would have made some bad decisions."

God's "No, your twin sister's not staying at the same college with you" led to "Thank you, God, for giving us a few years of individual experiences that let our relationship breathe and grow."

God's "No, you're not having a baby right now" led to "Thank you, God, that we saved this nest egg for delivery and can now sponsor twelve kids from Haiti."

God's "No, you aren't going to be a writer for the local newspaper like you wanted" led to "Thank you, God, that I get to write books, create journals, and point others to you!"

I think God says no to me more than I say it to my kids.

"Nos"can be brutal because if we prayed for something,

> It's easy to have faith when things go our way, but to trust him when things don't? Those are opportunities to glorify God like never before.

we really hoped it would happen. We pull back from God when we think he said no because he doesn't care, but "nos" are the very place we get to show God our faith. It's easy to have faith when things go our way, but to trust him when things don't? Those are opportunities to glorify God like never before.

Have you ever sung the words of the old hymn by Horatio Spafford when you got a no?

When peace, like a river, attendeth my way,
When sorrows like sea billows roll;
Whatever my lot, Thou hast taught me to say,
It is well, it is well, with my soul.[3]

I can't get through these lines without feeling the emotion. When I'm staring down circumstances I fought against and can *still* sing praise, I recognize my own devotion for God. I am reminded of how powerful a God he must be to capture my sinful heart and help me to respond with a maturity I could never muster on my own. It can only be God!

When I think about the story of Rahab, a Canaanite woman who was saved from destruction when the walls of Jericho came down (see Joshua 2–6), I always focus on the miracle of it all. She and her family were saved! She's part of the lineage of Jesus! How cool! Only recently did I stop to consider the devastation tangled in this miracle. Rahab lost her whole city and everything familiar to her. She lost every person she knew besides the loved ones within her four walls. She got a "yes" to her prayer to be saved, but it was buried under the rubble of a "no." Some miracles will be buried. If Rahab's only hope had been that Jericho wouldn't crumble to the ground, she could have missed out on God rescuing her family and welcoming them into his people.

God is at work in your life right now. There's a "yes" within the "no." Don't step away from God, but know that something is waiting under the rubble. Praise him. Look for him, even when you feel distant because he doesn't seem to be answering. Let your heart rejoice, knowing that this "no" may be making way for the very thing you praise him for in a future season. That may be one day on earth, but most definitely one day in heaven.

The Lord Never Makes a Mistake

The wilderness, deserts, and every rough terrain we walk through all feel like mistakes, don't they? They can't be part of the plan. Our limited minds can't understand this fully, but we can rest on the fact that God doesn't make mistakes. He is perfect and holy. He is right on time, never early.

If we commit to choosing God continuously through trials, we can avoid the kind of distance that we initiate, and we will see fruit from the unavoidable hard things that are for our own good and for God's purpose. When we throw off the weight of distance and draw near to God, we experience his comfort and see him working even in the hard times.

reflect ───────────────────────────────

Are there any choices you're making right now that are keeping you from intimacy with God?

Identify what you are currently waiting for and sprinkle "and the Lord was with me" throughout your description.

What fruit have you seen from any past "nos" from God?

read ───────────────────────────────

○ James 1:2-4
○ Isaiah 41:10

○ Romans 8:18
○ Psalm 66:10-12

9

I'm Good Now, but Want to Get the Next One?

Staying Dependent on the Mountaintop

WE LIVE FOR THE MOUNTAINTOP experiences in life—like when circumstances are going smoothly, we're at the top of our game, and relationships seem easy.

Sadly, most of us would take an easy season over a deepening relationship with God. How do I know this? Because I've done it. When I've entered an easy season, my prayers have started to trickle a little more slowly. The urgency hasn't been the same as it was in situations of depression, anxiety, or significant transition. And I've been so happy to be on the mountaintop that it hasn't bothered me too much to see my intimacy with God start to slip away. The mountaintop gives that false sense of *I got this, God. I'll catch you on the back nine when things start to fall apart again. Rest up and save your energy. . . . I'll be fine.*

There she is—the biggest lie I tell myself. Times when life feels good can give us a false sense of independence. How many of us find it easy to pray when we're desperate and in need but can go through a few good weeks forgetting to "check in" with God?

This is the weight of ease.

We miss out on celebrating with God in good times when we get too self-sufficient on the mountaintop.

I remember plopping in a bright pink chair in a hotel lobby before a big weekend for my company, Val Marie Paper. We were in the middle of a banner year. I wrote a book. I got to be a part of an amazing event I had been dreaming of for years. Our sales had nearly doubled. The family was great. Marriage solid. All good, right?

As I got ready to embark on another fun day of sharing our journals with new friends, I cracked open Deuteronomy 8. It's become my anthem in past mountaintop seasons, and I was preparing myself to waltz right into another. I had learned from past topples that the mountain is where people neglect God. It's where life feels comfortable again. If the valley can be summed up as me clinging to Jesus like a passenger on a bucking bronco, the ease of the mountain is me relaxing my grip. The unfortunate reality is that I get overconfident on the mountain. My pride leads me to believe that the ease I'm experiencing is something I've earned or created on my own.

It's amazing how overnight I can go from being hopelessly dependent on the Lord to get me through hard days to not even acknowledging his presence when things seem in my wheelhouse. Confidence is a funny thing. We praise confidence as king, but confidence in the wrong things can ruin us and make us forget that we are completely dependent on the Lord.

The ease of the mountaintop can be a weight that hinders our prayers. If we don't think we need God, we won't go to him. One of the greatest things we can do to grow our prayer lives is stay in a constant state of remembering just how dependent we are on God.

Deuteronomy 8 minces no words. We see Moses addressing the Israelites as they prepare to enter the Promised Land and begin living their best lives. Look at this description of where God is bringing them:

> For the LORD your God is bringing you into a
> good land, a land of brooks of water, of fountains
> and springs, flowing out in the valleys and hills, a
> land of wheat and barley, of vines and fig trees and
> pomegranates, a land of olive trees and honey, a
> land in which you will eat bread without scarcity, in
> which you will lack nothing, a land whose stones are
> iron, and out of whose hills you can dig copper. And
> you shall eat and be full, and you shall bless the Lord
> your God for the good land he has given you.
> DEUTERONOMY 8:7-10

The descriptions are eye-popping: milk and honey overflowing. Figs as far as the eye can see. And hills literally filled with copper. Yet God takes the opportunity to remind his people what he brought them out of because they start to forget.

We forget too.

In the midst of this beautiful description, God warns the Israelites about what might happen:

> Take care lest you forget the LORD your God by not
> keeping his commandments and his rules and his
> statutes, which I command you today, lest, when you
> have eaten and are full and have built good houses
> and live in them, and when your herds and flocks
> multiply and your silver and gold is multiplied and
> all that you have is multiplied, then your heart be
> lifted up, and you forget the LORD your God, who
> brought you out of the land of Egypt, out of the
> house of slavery.
> DEUTERONOMY 8:11-14

My judgy mind thinks, *How in the world could the people
not be reminded of God's hand as they surveyed such lush land?
First all the complaining when God freed them from slavery, and
now they're going to forget him altogether?*

Lord, help me. When I've surveyed the land of my own
lush life, I've had many a season of splendor where I forgot
the Lord too.

We like to peg God as he's depicted in the Old Testament
as vengeful. We think the New Testament is all grace and
the Old Testament is all wrath. But as I read God's warn-
ings here, I see grace. I see him like a parent grabbing our
hands before we plow into traffic. He knows the safe path
and clearly lets us know what it is.

How gracious is a God who reminds me that it's fool-
ish to save my prayer minutes for the next valley. I'm on an
unlimited talking plan with God, but the mountains leave
me vulnerable to pride and choosing my own way straight
into an unnecessary valley. I wonder how many mountaintop
seasons we leave early because we start making decisions on

our own instead of continuing to walk in obedience and close relationship with him.

It's strange that good things like springs and figs, happy toddlers, and good business years can become weights that hinder our prayers. But when we fix our eyes on them, they can. What's beautiful is that the mountaintop can be a place of such God-glorifying moments if we can keep our eyes on God amidst a shimmery copper mountain vying for our attention.

In Mark 6 we read two amazing accounts of Jesus: the feeding of the five thousand and Jesus walking on water. I'd call those two shimmering moments of Jesus' story. But in between, we find a transitional verse that tells another important story: "After [Jesus] had taken leave of them, he went up on the mountain to pray" (Mark 6:46).

I find it a bit odd. It seems like after turning five loaves of bread into enough to feed five thousand grown men plus women and children, you'd be riding pretty high. You'd feel so confident that you'd be floating on air. Instead, Jesus goes to the mountain to pray and then descends to the sea, where he walks on water. We don't know what he prayed about. Did he thank God? Ask God for strength for what was coming ahead? Lift up the disciples? I think it's okay we don't know his exact words. The point is that even in the middle of high highs, Jesus kept going to God. And if it was important for Jesus to commune with his Father at every turn, how important is it for us to do the same?

I remember in 2019 when my book *Grumpy Mom Takes a Holiday* was about to come out. I had wanted to be a writer since I was in middle school, and after a very messy and winding journey, I was finally living out my dream. In the midst of it, I was 100 percent aware that I might be tempted to casually tell God, "Hey! I got this one. Go ahead and take a nap or help that train wreck over there. I'll buzz you when the next hard thing comes."

Moments of triumph can do that to us, and I wasn't the only one aware. My husband and I surprised my publishers with a trip to their headquarters that winter. After we toured the office and talked about the book, Sarah, the associate publisher, and Kara, the acquisitions editor, volunteered to drive us back to our hotel. As we chatted, Sarah was kind enough to mention good qualities she saw in me. She also mentioned that she prayed for me to stay humble in the future as the book came out. This might sound strange, but I instantly felt loved by her prayers. She'd seen the pitfalls that success could bring authors, and she didn't want me to fall into them. Sarah didn't just want the book to succeed. She wanted me to succeed too.

This was like a Deuteronomy 8 moment.

Val, God has done amazing things in your life and story so far. Up ahead are lots of great things too. Don't forget who made them happen. When people forget, it's not pretty.

I won't say that remembering to stick close to God in the midst of good times is easy. On the steady days, putting off Bible time or prayer feels inconsequential. You're no longer a parched camel trying to quench your thirst. You're hydrated and feeling good, and one sip isn't going to change that. The problem isn't so much the missed sip but the overconfidence that makes us think we don't need anything else.

We aren't self-sufficient and never will be. We will always need God, even on the mountaintop. The devil would like to convince us that we can handle things without God, but we see how well that worked out for Eve in the Garden of Eden (see Genesis 3). And let's be honest, we've seen it in our own lives too.

Let's always stay needy, no matter how high the mountain. But how do we practically do that? Here are four ways to release the weight of ease.

1. Celebrate the Victory Longer

Psalm 18 is a victory psalm, written after the Lord delivered David from Saul's hand. If you've ever done a psalm-a-day reading plan, you've probably noticed that this is a long psalm. Fifty verses, to be exact. David spent a lot of time lamenting, as we discussed earlier, but this particular fifty-verse psalm is not full of lament, requests, or even confession. It's full of praise. David recounts the dire situation he was in, tells how he called out to God, and describes how God delivered him. As he exclaims about the Lord's power and how he triumphed over David's enemies, we can almost feel his joy and excitement.

I'll ask a tough question, and I know it's tough because I'd rather not answer it. When we think of prayer, do we picture this extended focus on praise? Do we spend fifty lines praising God for his victories in our lives? Or do we just give a nod of thanks and move on because we sort of expected him to answer? It's easy to get swept away by the next need in life rather than enjoying the spoils of victory. In business, experts talk often about making sure to celebrate the milestones.* Are we doing that in prayer? Or, as soon as we get the go-ahead on one request, do we launch into the next one?

---

*I'm terrible at this. I have spent many a big milestone day plugging away at the next thing.

What if we started sitting in the victory longer? What if the reason we forget God when we're on the mountaintop is because we're blazing through the victory?

I want to celebrate more moments with God. It's not just woo-woo gratitude. It has nothing to do with saying words because we think they will manifest something good in our future. Celebrating the victories prepares our hearts for surrender and obedience even when things are going so well that it doesn't look like we need to.

We need these moments of celebration in the valley because they remind us to have hope in who God is, but I think we need them just as much on the mountaintop because we need to remember our dependence.

2. Remember Who's Responsible

One key to keeping our eyes fixed on God on the mountaintop is remembering what he has done. Back in Deuteronomy 8, Moses' speech to the Israelites continues as he recounts some of the ways God has helped them:

> . . . who led you through the great and terrifying wilderness, with its fiery serpents and scorpions and thirsty ground where there was no water, who brought you water out of the flinty rock, who fed you in the wilderness with manna that your fathers did not know, that he might humble you and test you, to do you good in the end.
> DEUTERONOMY 8:15-16

Not only are we called to remember the past wilderness, but we should also recall its purpose. How did it change us? Why did we walk through it? Granted, many hard seasons aren't as easily defined as this one for the Israelites was. But even if we don't know exactly why we went through a tough situation, let us never forget how we even-

> **Who I am on the mountaintop will be different if I reflect on where I came from and who got me where I am.**

tually got to the mountain. If we don't remember whose hand guided us there, we'll likely get confused and take the credit.

Selah. That's worth pondering a little longer.

Moses continues with a warning for his people:

> Beware lest you say in your heart, "My power and the might of my hand have gotten me this wealth." You shall remember the LORD your God, for it is he who gives you power to get wealth, that he may confirm his covenant that he swore to your fathers, as it is this day. And if you forget the LORD your God and go after other gods and serve them and worship them, I solemnly warn you today that you shall surely perish.
> DEUTERONOMY 8:17-19

This is both beautiful and brutal. (I'll restrain myself from calling it brutiful.) Worshiping other gods feels a bit far-fetched in our modern day, but you know the things we idolize: our phones, our appearances, work that brings us praise and acclaim, others' approval of us through likes and comments on social media. It's brutal to imagine worshiping anyone but God but truly beautiful when we renounce those things that could capture our attention. Who I am on the mountaintop will be different if I reflect on where I came from and who got me where I am.

3. Be Present on the Mountain

It's hard to be content with the victory when we're waiting for the other shoe to drop. Those of us who are always looking for a good reason to worry don't need to be in a valley. If we're on the mountaintop, we'll just pre-worry for the next valley. The view is perfect for that. You know how they say that when you drive looking at the gutter, you'll eventually end up in it? It's possible to career down the mountain if you're staring at the next valley. Live in the moment with the Lord as best you can. The moments when I've experienced the most contentment have been when I've fought hard to be present on the mountaintop. I didn't question my worthiness of such a gift. (Gifts aren't earned anyway). I didn't wonder whether the blessings might actually be a trap like the Trojan horse. I simply sat in what was happening at that very moment.

The future gives us opportunities to be anxious. The past gives us opportunities to regret. But what if we toed the line, saw Jesus in the present, and enjoyed the gift of being on the mountain with him?

4. Bless Others

Victories are best shared. When we celebrate what God has done, it's basically like getting a promotion and buying everyone a round of drinks (okay, appetizers). The easy seasons aren't just for our benefit. Maybe God has plans to use us in them.

In the middle of a really burned-out season, we had someone unexpectedly offer us their lake house for a few days. I remember thinking how grateful I was that God had blessed them with that vacation home because we got to experience God's love through their generosity. If God wants to bless someone, he can do

> The easy seasons aren't just for our benefit. Maybe God has plans to use us in them.

it directly, but what a special thing that he often invites us to be a part of it! It blessed me to see someone give what they could have kept to themselves, and it inspired me to do the same.

One of my goals the last few years has been to have more room in our home so we can invite the chaos of others in. It seems counterintuitive to want chaos, but it also sounds amazing to have space to love and serve others so well.

When we found out both my twin sister and my sister-in-law were pregnant and due just three weeks apart, my husband teased that we needed to have another baby too. I took it overly seriously and gave him my very spiritual reason for what I felt the Lord was calling us to in the next season. Life with a four- and seven-year-old has been amazing. We're out of the baby and toddler fog. And now we get to help two family members about to enter into it. So often it feels like we're faced with problems in the lives of everyone around us while simultaneously battling our own problems. What if the mountaintop wasn't seen just as a retreat from challenges but also as an opportunity to bless others?

These four ways to throw off the weight of ease—celebrating the victories longer, remembering what God has done, being present on the mountain, and blessing others when we're in a good place—have something in common. They take the attention off ourselves. We aren't bemoaning our mess-ups in the valley, and we aren't inflating our contributions to the mountaintop. We're simply doing what our key verse for the book calls us to do and fixing our eyes on Jesus (Hebrews 12:1).

If we can do this, we don't have to fear the good times. We can stop assuming that the mountaintop is where our prayers fade or where we try to do everything on our own. We can also stop fearing the valleys to come. There will be more, but we've been logging lots of time with our heavenly Father and are ready for what's next.

As I sat in that plush pink hotel lobby chair a few years ago reflecting on Deuteronomy 8, I was hopeful for the mountain I thought I was about to ascend. Whoops . . . my mistake. The mountain I was expecting turned out to be more like a plateau. But I was so sure of God in this season and so grateful for all he had done in previous seasons that it didn't rattle me or derail my prayers. I'm confident that if I had walked into that weekend without inviting God to ascend the mountain with me, I would have tumbled down only to cry out to God to come rescue me. Instead, he was beside me holding my hand and pulling me away from the edge just like a parent pulls a kid out of traffic. I'm glad I did the mountain with God.

Mountaintop experiences don't have to weigh down our prayer lives. Let's instead enjoy them with the victor and let the mountain remind us where our help comes from, just as the psalmist reflects: "I lift up my eyes to the mountains—where does my help come from? My help comes from the LORD, the Maker of heaven and earth" (Psalm 121:1-2, NIV).

When we throw off the weight of ease, we get to enjoy uninterrupted moments with our generous God.

reflect —————————————————————

What amazing gifts from God have captured your attention and even become a hindrance to your intimacy with him?

What would it look like to be present in your next mountain-top experience?

Ask the Lord, "Where can I bless others?"

read ————————————————————————

- ○ Psalm 44:3
- ○ James 5:13
- ○ Isaiah 52:7
- ○ John 15:5-8
- ○ Psalm 115:1

10

Can You Fit in This Box?

Learning the Power of Living in God's Presence

WHAT'S THE BIGGEST answered prayer you've ever experienced? A few things come to mind in my life, some of which I've shared in the pages of this book. I'm embarrassed to admit that most revolve around me having the kind of life I wanted. I've talked to so many other people in the same boat. Our biggest answered prayers are the child we prayed for or the dream job we got. They might even involve the healing of a loved one or the restoration of a marriage. These are valuable things, but they're all about us, and I fear we're stopping short.

I've read a lot of books on prayer, many of which are decades or even centuries old, and I've seen stories of revival, salvation for the lost, and insanely momentous moves. Just the other day, I read the story of a man who went to Russia for a month because he felt God leading him to pray. He told his friend, "I'm to pray that God will shake all of Russia. I'll ask Him to use current events—whatever they are—to shake what can be shaken, so doors will be open to the Gospel and believers will have new freedom to worship." He prayed for thirty-one days, and the day after he left, the nuclear power plant explosion at Chernobyl happened. This event, while horribly devastating, also brought a spark of hope. Since the increased radiation levels were detectable all the way in Sweden, the Russian government was unable to keep the event a secret. It forced *glasnost*, or openness, and became a turning point in bringing freedom to the people of the USSR. Just two years later, laws about religious freedom in Russia started changing.[1]

Can we imagine God entrusting us to pray for something like that—something that affects a whole group of people or even a nation? What is it that God wants to do in our generation that we're too busy focusing on our own lives to pray for?

As I get ready to turn in this book, I'm making frequent pit stops to check the news. We're a month away from the 2020 presidential election. We're experiencing intense social unrest. And what hasn't been destroyed in wildfires or hurricanes is empty because of the coronavirus.

Is God trying to get our attention? Is God calling us outside our own walls? Not only that, but is God calling us to see *him* outside the four walls we put him in? Is he reminding us that he is so much bigger and more powerful than we often imagine when we're praying?

This is the weight of compartmentalizing.

We miss out on the fullness of God when we pigeon-hole him into the places we expect him to fit.

If we try to minimize God's power and presence by thinking of him mainly as one who can improve our circumstances, we will never be able to experience everything God has for us in our prayer lives. If your God is too small for you to bring him the big things or if you only think to talk to him at mealtimes or on Sundays, you'll feel like there must be more to prayer—because there is.

I want us to throw off all the faulty thinking that puts God in a box and instead rediscover who he is.

Focus on the Eternal, not the Temporary

It's painful to see those areas where we've made our prayer lives all about us. Desiring prayer feels holy, but somehow I've desired prayer only for what it will do for my temporary circumstances. I want guidance and clarity for where to go next—partly because I want to follow God's will, but mostly because I don't want the frustration of indecision or not knowing. I want God's presence—partly because I want to know God, but mostly because I just want the peace and joy that come with it. I want a nice house—partly because I want to be hospitable and disciple others, but mostly because I want a comfy place where I can retreat.

This might be the chapter that breaks us. We all want to skip this awkward part of the conversation on prayer, but we can't if we're tired of missing out on power-filled prayers. Our focus on the temporary might be why it keeps happening.

Is God only good at giving out Band-Aids of comfort for the here and now, or does he have the power to make things new for eternity? Let's go back to the verse we read when we started this book:

Therefore, since we are surrounded by so great a cloud of witnesses, let us also lay aside every weight, and sin which clings so closely, and let us run with endurance the race that is set before us, looking to Jesus, the founder and perfecter of our faith, who for the joy that was set before him endured the cross, despising the shame, and is seated at the right hand of the throne of God.

HEBREWS 12:1-2

Prayer is our most practical way of getting out of the temporary and getting into the eternal.

According to Josephus, a first-century Jewish historian, "prizes often were set before athletes as motivation" when they competed.[2] For Jesus, the prize was eternity. If we have any hope of running this race well, it's going to be because we kept our eyes on eternity too. It's not going to be because we focused only on the world we could see.

tip

If you're looking for things to pray for beyond your own comfort, try these!

- Salvation for the lost
- Refining during hard times
- Revival in our nation and world
- God's Word to reach the ends of the earth
- Eyes to see what God sees
- Faithfulness in mundane tasks
- To remember God's Word in daily life

Prayer is our most practical way of getting out of the temporary and getting into the eternal, but sometimes we treat God like our sidekick on earth instead of stepping into *his* presence and getting a glimpse of eternity.

Revelation 21:3-4 paints a beautiful picture we can cling to:

I heard a loud voice from the throne saying, "Behold, the dwelling place of God is with man. He will dwell with them, and they will be his people, and God himself will be with them as their God. He will wipe away every tear from their eyes, and death shall be no more, neither shall there be mourning, nor crying, nor pain anymore, for the former things have passed away."

How many times have I prayed for relief in this minute or hour but have forgotten what will last forever? When we focus on eternity, we remember who God is, and suddenly our reality becomes much bigger.

Remember He's Not My Pocket God

Praying to a God who cares about little old me is pretty wild. In the past, I may have twisted things up a bit and made the Lord my personal God. Not personal in the sense that he cared about me and we could have an intimate relationship—that's accurate. I was using the term in the same sense as in personal CD player, personal computer, or personal assistant. I thought of God as being at my disposal. Yikes. I'm uncomfortable just typing that.

Part of living for more than our comforts is seeing God for who he is. Paul David Tripp writes, "If you're not living in awe of God, you are left with no higher agenda than to live for yourself. . . . If I am at the center, I will define good as what is comfortable, predictable, pleasurable, natural, and easy. The good life will be the easy life because awe of self will have replaced it."[3]

We desperately want to understand God fully because if we can't, how can we trust him? So we personalize him. We casually say, "Hey, God," as if we're texting a friend to ask a favor. We call him "Papa" or "Daddy" without remembering that he's more than that. Of course we need to see him as father, but we never want to mute his power. The God we get to pray to is Father *and* King.

So, in this section, we're going to get a real good look at how big God is.

> The LORD said to Moses, "Go to the people and consecrate them today and tomorrow. Have them wash their clothes and be ready by the third day, because on that day the LORD will come down on Mount Sinai in the sight of all the people. Put limits for the people around the mountain and tell them, 'Be careful that you do not approach the mountain or touch the foot of it. Whoever touches the mountain is to be put to death.'"
> EXODUS 19:10-12, NIV

This passage gives me a visual of a powerful and mighty God—one so holy that the Israelites couldn't approach his mountain and had to prepare themselves to even be in his presence. Is this really the God we're praying to?

A. W. Tozer wrote, "You know what we've done? We've

brought God down until nobody can respect Him anymore."⁴ We've tried so hard to understand God that we've come to view him as smaller than he is. It's hard to comprehend how a loving God could say that anyone who touched the mountain had to be put to death, so we soften the edges of his power. Have I softened God so I feel comfortable with him? What we might see as mean or cruel is sheer holiness that we simply cannot comprehend.

It's easy to see God as either powerful and distant *or* personal and muted. Most of us have chosen the latter. When you get up close to God and develop an intimate relationship with him, it's almost scary to remember how powerful he is. It's like getting comfortable petting a furry animal we assume to be a docile kitty and then suddenly recognizing that it's actually a tiger.

We don't have to fear God's power because he is good. If we can reconcile those things and come to him in prayer remembering what he is capable of, I wonder what we'll see in our prayer lives. Surely something more than the sleepy prayer times I've often experienced.

Does this sound familiar? The sun isn't up yet, and neither is my family. I stumble to my favorite chair to read my Bible. I'm waiting for my pat on the back from God as he marvels at my sacrifice. I mean, it's so early! What happens next is so methodical that I hardly even remember who I'm talking to, but he is getting an earful about the dreads of my day. Even though I'm the one talking, the present conversation isn't enough

If you want to change your prayer life in an instant, take two minutes to think about *who* you're praying to.

to stave off my sleepiness, so I succumb. I eventually wake up to the noise of kids coming down the hall.

Where's the power?

If you want to change your prayer life in an instant, take two minutes to think about *who* you're praying to. Really think about it.

- The God whose words created the earth and sky
- The God who breathed life into bones and dust
- The God who dreamed up penguins and tulips
- The God who shaped mountains and beaches
- The God who formed billions of people, no two the same (I'm a twin and still know this is true)
- The God who hears every prayer no matter how many happen at once (a fact that boggled my childhood brain at bedtime prayers)
- The God who is outside time and on a heavenly throne
- The God who spoke to prophets in the Old Testament and fulfilled more than three hundred prophecies with Jesus' life and death
- The God who is more consistent than the sunrise and more unconditional than a mother's love

That's who we get to pray to. That's the God who wants to speak to us if we'll spare a second to listen. That's the God who wants to respond to our requests. That's the God who invites us over and over again in Scripture to pray and tells us to pray without ceasing.

The following question may be obvious, but our answer to it can alter our lives and change how we pray: *What God are you praying to?*

This is our God!

Psalm 29

> Ascribe to the LORD, O heavenly beings,
> > ascribe to the LORD glory and strength.
> Ascribe to the LORD the glory due his name;
> > worship the LORD in the splendor of holiness.
>
> The voice of the LORD is over the waters;
> > the God of glory thunders,
> > the LORD, over many waters.
> The voice of the LORD is powerful;
> > the voice of the LORD is full of majesty.
>
> The voice of the LORD breaks the cedars;
> > the LORD breaks the cedars of Lebanon.
> He makes Lebanon to skip like a calf,
> > and Sirion like a young wild ox.
>
> The voice of the LORD flashes forth flames of fire.
> The voice of the LORD shakes the wilderness;
> > the LORD shakes the wilderness of Kadesh.
>
> The voice of the LORD makes the deer give birth
> > and strips the forests bare,
> > and in his temple all cry, "Glory!"
>
> The LORD sits enthroned over the flood;
> > the LORD sits enthroned as king forever.
> May the LORD give strength to his people!
> > May the LORD bless his people with peace!

If your prayers feel lackluster and narrow, pause before you start praying, and spend a little time identifying who you're talking to. Prayer can sometimes feel like talking to the ceiling, but two minutes of thinking about who God really is makes my voice tremble when I get a glimpse of the power I'm inviting into my life.

Live in God's Ongoing Presence

When I was first learning how to pray, I would ask the Lord in the morning to be with me throughout the day. It was a pretty great thing to pray, if I do say so myself. The thing is, I didn't give it a second thought until each night like clockwork, when my head hit the pillow and I'd be reminded of that morning prayer. It felt light-years away.

As we talk about prayer, it's easy to assign it some nice, tidy spots in our calendars and our lives. Mine are in the mornings before the girls wake up, for sure at the table before dinner, and possibly at night if we're feeling really holy. There. Plan made. What a great consistent life of prayer I've got!

When our second daughter was born, my morning routine was blown to bits. And we absolutely weren't praying around the table for dinner, because I don't even remember dinners at that point. I didn't starve, of course, so I'm sure I ate somehow, but we certainly weren't seated neatly around the table thanking the good Lord for another meal. And possibly at night? Actually, I had that down consistently, but it was typically "Dear Lord, I see her stirring on the monitor. She just lifted her head. She's about to cry. She's about to cry. Nooooooo! Make it stop, Lord!"

If I'm honest, I'd prided myself on the solid time I was able to give to the Lord each morning when I had one child.

Quiet, intentional time with the Lord is obviously still necessary at any stage of life, but focusing *only* on this meant I totally missed what it was to live in God's presence.

High school Valerie was on to something when she prayed to walk with God throughout the day. It took me two decades to grasp what that looked like, but now that I do, I know that my goal is no longer to pray more. That may sound bad, but what I'm really after is time in the Lord's presence. I want to know him. To abide in him.

Up until a few years ago, I was demanding that thirty minutes or even an hour with God in the morning carry me through the next twenty-four hours. I found myself so frustrated that I could have these amazing quiet times so filled with the Spirit and then a few hours later forget all about him and lose that joy and peace.

Seeking the Lord's ongoing presence isn't about marking another thing off your to-do list. It's about being so awake to God's love and grace that our only response is to want more of him. It's about realizing that he's already with us; we simply need to look for him and stop choosing worthless things. The

tip ───────────────────────────────

When you need to remember who God really is, pray through some of these verses:

- 2 Samuel 7:22
- Job 26:7-14
- Psalm 145:3
- Psalm 147:4-5
- Jeremiah 10:12

- 1 Corinthians 6:14
- Ephesians 1:19-21
- Ephesians 3:20
- Colossians 2:12

morning approach I thought was abundant before was really like eating a big breakfast and nothing else throughout the day. I'd slowly feel the hunger creep in until I was famished. And you know when you are so hungry that you no longer want to eat? That often happened in my prayer life too.

I remember a season of feeling pretty far from God. I didn't have any gigantic skeletons in my closet, but I made lots of little decisions to keep checking out celebrity gossip or closely following that Instagram influencer in place of spending time with the Creator of the universe. One day, after dropping my girls off at school, I felt desperate to simply do life with God. So I pulled out what I can only assume is an elementary-level exercise: I visualized God sitting with me in the car, ready to engage in conversation with me. It was overwhelming. I know God hears my prayers, but to envision having his full attention made it so real. It was no longer a hypothetical "If you could ask God anything, what would you say?" moment. He was here, just like he always had been, but I was finally awake to it. In an instant, heaven came down. Things that had mattered moments before, like a busy workday or cranky toddler, didn't matter in light of eternity because I was sitting with the Creator of the universe.

In its simplest terms, spending time with God is just being aware of him no matter what we're doing in the tangible world. We can experience his presence as we work or take care of kids. As David wrote, "You know when I sit and when I rise; you perceive my thoughts from afar" (Psalm 139:2, NIV).

If we want to experience the fullness of the Lord, we cannot limit our time with him to our comfy quiet-time chair or Sundays at church. What happens in the mundane moments with God throughout our week could transform our daily lives if we actively pursue that time in his presence. Folding laundry while wrapped up in a conversation with God or worshiping while I cook opens my eyes to eternity in the moments I may feel the furthest from it. God is not limited by a building or by whether our hands are free, so we don't need to limit ourselves either.

Let Our Lives Flow from Time with God

Earlier this year, I felt convicted to live a life that flows from prayer. I wanted my time with God to affect every decision I made and every thought I had. That's a tall order for prayer, but I think that's why the Bible talks about praying without ceasing.

John Onwuchekwa says, "When prayer is sparse and sporadic, when it's done just enough to ease the conscience and not much more, we've got a problem."[5] The idea of praying "to ease the conscience" sounds awful, but I know it's possible. I've prayed when I wanted a quick hit of peace after I read about something anxiety-inducing going on in our world. I've made a little extra time with God after it's been a while—just enough to avoid guilt or shame about the lopsided time I spend on worldly pursuits.

Here's where we separate the prayer dabblers from the prayer warriors. Is our goal to do the bare minimum? Blessing our dinner. Bowing our heads in church. Keeping God safely in the compartments we've built for him. Or do we want to truly live the way the Word calls us to when it says to pray without ceasing?

What does this phrase actually mean? We know it can't possibly mean we pray without stopping because we've got to interact with others, earn a living, and follow directions to new places without getting in a wreck. The idea of praying without ceasing shows up in several verses:

- Colossians 4:2—"*Continue steadfastly in prayer*, being watchful in it with thanksgiving" (emphasis added).

- Romans 12:12—"Rejoice in hope, be patient in tribulation, *be constant in prayer*" (emphasis added).

- Ephesians 6:18—"*Praying at all times* in the Spirit, with all prayer and supplication. To that end, keep alert with all perseverance, making supplication for all the saints" (emphasis added).

- 1 Thessalonians 5:17—"*Pray without ceasing*" (emphasis added).

The Bible Exposition Commentary says we are "to 'keep the receiver off the hook' and be in touch with God so that our praying is part of a long conversation that is not broken." It also says it means "we should be constantly in fellowship with God so that prayer is as normal to us as breathing."[6] *As normal to us as breathing* sounds amazing, doesn't it?

Another way I'd put it is keeping a short tether with the Lord, living in a deep awareness that he's right there on the other side of the phone line. And the phone isn't lost under your bed somewhere, either. It's one of those old corded phones, where the short length of the cord keeps you within arm's reach.

As I read those four verses above, I also noticed that sometimes prayer correlates with an ongoing need for discernment that could only come from continuous prayer. Colossians 4:2 says to be "*watchful*" (emphasis added). Romans 12:11-12 says, "*Do not be slothful* in zeal, be fervent in spirit, serve the Lord. Rejoice in hope, be patient in tribulation, be constant in prayer" (emphasis added). Ephesians 6:18 says to "*keep alert*." First Thessalonians 5 gets a bit wordier but says,

> We urge you, brothers, admonish the idle, encourage the fainthearted, help the weak, be patient with them all. See that no one repays anyone evil for evil, but *always seek* to do good to one another and to everyone. Rejoice always, pray without ceasing, give thanks in all circumstances; for this is the will of God in Christ Jesus for you. Do not quench the Spirit. Do not despise prophecies, but *test everything*; hold fast what is good. Abstain from every form of evil.
> VERSES 14-22, EMPHASIS ADDED

Maybe I'm making a leap here, but as I read these passages, I can't help but notice they all feature a string of challenges for believers to live holy lives. And that's simply not possible if we aren't abiding in the Lord. Not just dabbling in prayer but coming consistently to his throne.

Our ongoing conversation with the Lord doesn't look like having our heads bowed and hands folded 24-7. Instead, it involves including God in the way that we think, which—as I learned when I recently studied the brain—has incredible bearing on what we believe, how we speak, and what we do. Perhaps "praying without ceasing" looks less like the desperate prayers we throw up throughout our days and more like taking each thought captive and examining it *with* the Lord.

What if we lived in constant awareness that we are present with God? How different would life be? Would we ditch the lies faster? Would we experience less fear, since challenges appear smaller in God's presence?

I 100 percent promise you that God knew what was coming in our world today when he called us to pray without ceasing. He knew we'd be busy. He knew our homes would be loud. But more than anything, he knew that our lives would be radically different if we were paying attention to his presence.

As I talked this chapter over with Kara, my right-hand gal for Val Marie Paper, she said something so profound: "If you have time to think, you have time to pray." Taking thoughts captive with God and turning those thoughts toward God *is* life in his presence. For me, it looks like taking a second to think rationally about a sudden pain rather than assuming it's a death sentence.* For you, it may mean looking at your bank account and not tailspinning into panic, because you recognize that your Creator sees exactly what you're facing and will provide. And we're never too busy for that. You've got time, friend. I know that doesn't make it easy all of a sudden, but hopefully it will fill you with hope and an anticipation for every opportunity to pray without ceasing.

This is what we experience when we say yes to time in God's presence. When we throw off the weight of compartmentalizing, stop trying to put God in a box, and welcome him into every moment, we experience his fullness. Psalm 16:11 tells us, "You make known to me the path of life; in your presence there is fullness of joy; at your right hand are pleasures forevermore."

---

*I can be a hypochondriac. I jump really far, guys.

reflect

Where have you compartmentalized God? Where are you not experiencing God in your day?

Are there any characteristics of God you have softened to better understand him? Talk to a trusted friend about these areas so you can confidently pray to our all-powerful and loving God.

Think of a specific mundane or hard moment. How could it have been different if it had been walked out in the presence of the Lord?

read

- Romans 12:2
- Matthew 6:33
- Romans 8:5
- Proverbs 4:23

11

Am I Fighting the Right Things?

Engaging in My Real Spiritual Battle

I CAN'T SLEEP TONIGHT. The last few weeks have held many fitful nights, the scariest dreams of my life, and spiritual turmoil. I'm dreading sleep because I know what I have to look forward to. In my middle-of-the-night stupor, I somehow pieced together what I was witnessing—a spiritual battle. It's hard to explain, but it feels like I woke up in the middle of surgery and wasn't supposed to see what I saw. I don't mean to sound dramatic. I didn't have any strong visuals, just an uneasiness that there was a spiritual battle happening. Two sides were at war, and I somehow stumbled upon the action.*

Spiritual battle or spiritual warfare sounds like a swirly concept that glides right over my head, but it's actually

---

*If that feels too heavy too fast, just imagine your toys waking up like in *Toy Story*. Suddenly you figure out there's a whole other dimension to life that you didn't realize existed.

simple: What looks like the battle—people we don't like, circumstances that don't go our way, or even our own seeming lack of willpower—isn't the actual battle. Underneath the surface of this temporary earth, the devil, who made himself an enemy of God because he wanted to be God, fights to defeat him. Spoiler alert: God will take the victory, but that doesn't stop the

God will take the victory, but that doesn't stop the devil from throwing punches on his way out.

devil from throwing punches on his way out.

As I washed makeup off my face this evening, dreading another restless night, John 10:10 came to my mind: "The thief comes only to steal and kill and destroy. I came that they may have life and have it abundantly." The devil's only desire is to sabotage us and take from us.

Spiritual warfare is where I engage in a response.

If you're anything like most believers, you likely forget there's a spiritual battle going on. We have a world of distractions that keep our feet so firmly planted on earth that we forget what's happening around us. We get distracted by after-school activities, new jobs, big moves, and challenging people. And because of that, we don't engage in the spiritual war around us.

This is the weight of sideshows.

We miss out on winning spiritual battles in prayer against our actual enemy when we waste time and energy on the wrong fight.

When we understand the real battle we need to fight and realize that prayer is the way we do it, we will find victory and experience power-filled prayers to our Father that go far beyond our requests for a good night's sleep or a blessed meal.

This is the reality: The enemy comes to steal our peace, kill our joy, and destroy our hope, but God comes that we may have abundant life! He's like a knight in shining armor, galloping to the rescue. It's less cheesy than that, but in this moment, as I type words to be read by a weary pray-er who's fighting a very real spiritual battle, I want it to be clear that you have an actual Savior. A God who saves. *Savior* isn't Jesus' nickname. *First name, Jesus; last name, Christ; but some people like to call me Savior.* No, the name *Savior* describes what Jesus came to do for you and me. And when we're in the battle, we need to lean into how heroic he is.

He doesn't demand that we be the heroes. Our job is to make sure we're fighting the right enemy through prayer and not trying to fight alone. Here are four things we have to remember so we don't get sidetracked.

1. That's Not My Enemy

Prayer is inviting God to fight on our behalf. A spiritual battle is not going to be won with brute strength. It's going to be won on our knees. But too many times, when we're battling discouragement, despair, fear, or overwhelming obstacles, we forget that the battle is spiritual, and we try to fight in other ways.

It can happen when we face hardships that require refuge in Jesus but we try to distract ourselves with worldly things or we downplay what's happening.

It can happen when we find ourselves drifting from the Lord and chalk it up to a slight shift that we don't think will really make any difference.

It can happen when we let mistakes ruin a relationship because instead of seeing the devil as our enemy, we see our sister in Christ as the enemy.

Remembering our real enemy changes everything.

Ephesians 6:12 says, "For we do not wrestle against flesh and blood, but against the rulers, against the authorities, against the cosmic powers over this present darkness, against the spiritual forces of evil in the heavenly places." If the battle were against flesh and blood, maybe some of our tactics would work. But this isn't a flesh-and-blood battle, and if we try to fight that way, is it any wonder we're all so worn out? When I feel tension in the world, I'm so guilty of getting defensive with those I perceive as my enemies. I spend precious time hurling rocks at what I think is the problem, only to feel too defeated and worn out to even pray.

But prayer is our first and most important line of defense. It's the only way to fight when the enemy hides behind everyday things.

Our enemy is not our anxiety.

Our enemy is not a political party.

Our enemy is not our business competition.

Our enemy is not even the guy who cut us off in traffic and is *very* proud of his loud truck.

Our enemy is an evil and prideful being determined to drag everyone he can down with him.

2. That's Not My Goal

To be honest, I hesitated to write this book because I knew the spiritual warfare that could come. And it most definitely did not disappoint. Every season of big, monumental God moments in my life has been met with an enemy very determined to throw me off. I had to ask myself tough questions: *Will I not do what I feel the Lord calling me to because I'm scared of Satan? Do I think he is more powerful than God?* I knew that isn't true, so I couldn't let him sideline me.

If we attempt anything for the Kingdom the enemy's claws come out.

And, sweet friend, if you're doing good work for the Kingdom of God, the devil is after you, trying to get you to quit. He might shout lies that your sin, your busy schedule, or your brood of kids disqualifies you. He might convince you that you should get more education before you start talking about God or that you should keep quiet altogether.

The ironic part is your life may even look like a mess. You might look like a faithless Christian who just can't learn how to banish anxiety and trust God for good. You might look like a backslider who keeps falling for sins you thought you dealt with years ago. I know fruit and growth speak to God's work in our lives, but I think sometimes those rough patches in our spiritual walks speak to how unrelenting the devil is because he sees what we might do for God and is nervous to let us run wild.

The straitlaced believer who keeps to herself and is glad she bought her ticket to heaven early but has no plans to invite anyone else? Why would the devil even bother throwing a stick in the spokes of her life? But a dedicated follower of Jesus who wants to be involved in growing his Kingdom? That's a different story. This is not a PSA telling you to hush so you don't get hurt. That's not our goal. This is an invitation to get in the fight because that's where we get to see God work.

The battle isn't evidence that you should retreat or lie low for a while. It's a reminder that what you are doing gives the father of lies a chill down the spine-tingliest spine in the world. The enemy isn't going down easy if you are fighting for Jesus, the orphans, or the widows. If you're preaching unity and reconciliation or being a voice for victims of sex trafficking, expect roadblocks, discouragement, opposition, and moments of self-doubt. If you're on a mission to share Jesus with a neighbor, don't be surprised by cancellations and more obstacles than should be normal for getting together for coffee. Accept that this will happen, and commit to responding with prayer.

By now you know I like asking the tough questions—the ones that crush my own toes too. But I have to ask: Are we really wrestling "spiritual forces of evil"? Or has life gotten so cozy that the enemy wouldn't even bother to engage us? Do we blend into the world so much that the devil doesn't even realize we're a threat to his plans?

We don't need to poke the bear to prove we're doing God's work. We simply need to ask the Lord to reveal if there's anything that he's called us to do that we've been too comfortable to engage in. And then we pray for the courage to do it.

3. This Isn't My Battle

Last night, I could feel the tightness in my chest as I tossed and turned. The last few weeks have been filled with mistakes and setbacks leading up to a big product launch for our company. I had recently felt like God was calling us to challenge people to stretch their prayer lives in big ways, and y'all know our enemy doesn't like that. The product we created was what I hoped would be the next step for so many women ready to hear God speak into their lives—not just through answered prayers but through small whispers because their ears were tuned to his voice.

The thing is, even though I was covering the situation with prayer, I wasn't feeling any spiritual victory over it. As I prayed, I noticed how my thoughts were stuck on the problem. *Val, you just prayed for fifteen minutes, and you are* still *missing how big God is. You're still focused on the problem,* I thought to myself.

When I finally got up from my middle-of-the-night stirring, I flipped open my Bible to a spot where I had stuck a sticky note—Psalm 83. I don't love this method of choosing Scripture, but this seems to be my middle-of-the-night approach. I knew I needed the Word in me to align my heart with truth, and I wasn't picky about what specific passage it was. I started reading:

O God, do not keep silence;
> do not hold your peace or be still, O God!
For behold, *your enemies* make an uproar;
> those who *hate you* have raised their heads.
They lay crafty plans *against your people*;
> they consult together against your treasured ones.
PSALM 83:1-3, EMPHASIS ADDED

Three verses into Psalm 83, I saw Asaph, the writer, talk to God about "your enemies" and how they were threatening "your people." Then I realized something I had forgotten in all this struggle: For weeks, I had been trying to fight a battle that wasn't mine to win.

I wish you could have seen the pressure roll off my back in that moment. The issues weren't gone, but it was like I was handing over the keys to God. I stopped pretending that this was a battle I was responsible for winning. My enemy,

When you realize it's not technically your battle, you realize you aren't fighting alone. the devil, is really God's enemy. And God is already fighting him.

When you realize it's not technically your battle, you realize you aren't fighting alone. You aren't responsible for all the answers. You aren't responsible for bringing your own equipment. Your job is to show up through prayer and release the results to God.

See how Asaph continues in the Psalm:

> They say, "Come, let us wipe them out as a nation;
>   let the name of Israel be remembered no more!"
> For they conspire with one accord;
>   against you they make a covenant . . .
>
> Do to them as you did to Midian,
>   as to Sisera and Jabin at the river Kishon, . . .
> Make their nobles like Oreb and Zeeb,
>   all their princes like Zebah and Zalmunna, . . .
>
> O my God, make them like whirling dust,
>   like chaff before the wind.
> As fire consumes the forest,
>   as the flame sets the mountains ablaze,
> so may you pursue them with your tempest
>   and terrify them with your hurricane!
> PSALM 83:4-15

He is calling on the Lord to fight this battle. He's rattling off a roll call of God's recent victories. As I read this passage, my voice gets louder and my pace quickens because, as I recall the victories, I feel the strength of the one I'm inviting to fight on my behalf.

In that late-night moment, though, I had to admit that my prayers hadn't been sounding like this. They sounded much more like "God, can you help me out? I've got this battle, and it's really hard, and I'm lost without you." There was some dependence on the Lord there, but in all my prayers, it's still been *my* battle to fight. I was just seeking a good strong ally.

Asaph, though, got it. The battle was not his. This battle I'm facing is not mine, either. This is the Lord's.

Can you imagine if we lived our lives remembering without a doubt that Satan's main enemy is not us but God—the God who fights for us? When I realized this, my prayers became less like cries of "Lord, help me! I'm drowning here!" and more like cries of "I'm ready for battle, sir!"

God has called us to the fight, but we're not the strategists or the commanding officers. We're just the foot soldiers, following orders to pray. William Cowper said,

Satan trembles when he sees
the weakest saint upon his knees.[1]

Don't you just love that? I can do that. I can keep going to God in prayer when the battle rages.

4. Those Aren't My Weapons

If we're going to go to battle, we need the proper equipment. The weapons I pick up when I'm left to my own devices aren't working.

I wield a sword of harsh words that cut other people deep.

I put on the helmet of isolation and don't let others in.

I shield myself by zoning out on my phone for "me time."

I assume the fetal position, already accepting defeat instead of being firmly battle-ready.

I even pick up some silly toy or distraction in hopes of denying the battle altogether.

I know what you're thinking: *We're talking spiritual weapons? She's for sure heading to the Armor of God passage in Ephesians 6.*

We'll get there, wise grasshopper. Kind of. As I studied Ephesians recently, I noticed that Paul talked a ton about the relationship between the earth and the spiritual world. I ended up with nineteen little boxes around words like *heavenly places, cosmic power, eternal,* and more. The other theme I noticed concerned our relationship to God as children. I ended up with eighteen little circles around words like *heirs, inheritance, riches, adoption,* and even *seated* (emphasizing our relationship to God).

If we're going to know why it's important to clothe ourselves in the armor of God, we have to see Ephesians 6 in light of the entire book. How amazing that the chapters before this famous passage root us in the truths that we're God's kids, that he gives us everything we need, and that the four-dimensional world we live in, touch, and see is not all there is. The weapons identified in Ephesians 6 are God's weapons—identified as "the belt of truth," "the breastplate of righteousness," the shoes of "the gospel of peace," "the shield of faith," "the helmet of salvation," and "the sword of the Spirit" (verses 14-17). They're other-worldly and provided for us.*

The weapons I mentioned earlier—harsh words, isolation, zoning out, and so forth—can't be my weapons. Why? Because they're weak and limited. They're just things I dreamed up on my own. And when I'm forging my own weapons, I'm stuck in my own mind. Rick Renner writes, "The mind is the strategic center where the battle is won or lost in spiritual warfare!"[2] The mind is where the action begins. It's where our enemy plants seeds of discontentment, disbelief, discord, and disobedience. He makes us think the ideas originated with us.

Our enemy cannot make us do anything, but he can tempt us to do everything. This is why, repeatedly throughout Scripture, we're told to "take every thought captive" (2 Corinthians 10:5) or "be transformed by the renewal of your mind" (Romans 12:2). First Peter 1:13 even says, "Therefore, preparing your minds for action, and being sober-minded, set your hope fully on the grace that will be brought to you at the revelation of Jesus Christ."

Prayer is so important in this battle because we need to renew our thinking in the truth of Christ. When we come into his presence, we're able to remember our identity in Christ. We're able to remember who we're really fighting and that the battle is going on in our minds. We're reminded to keep resisting the devil so that he will flee (see James 4:7). We're able to remember who's already won the victory.

---

*We won't break down the whole Armor of God in this chapter. Priscilla Shirer has a powerful study called *The Armor of God* that I highly recommend even for those already familiar with the passage.

The Power We Have

Before we wrap up this chapter, I want to make it abundantly clear that we have enormous power in Christ for the spiritual battle that rages. Normally things that have big payoffs require enormous energy, but this requires so little of us besides turning to the Lord in prayer. Major victory in our spiritual battles simply requires making ourselves available to fight in prayer and in our minds against the enemy's schemes.

In the midst of my own fitful nights, I remember reading that author and prayer warrior Evelyn Christenson saw sleepless nights as a call to pray. She felt that God was looking for willing hearts to engage in the battle, and she believed that God woke her up because he knew she'd pray. One night, she felt the Lord prompting her to pray for her friend Jacque. Evelyn later discovered that in those moments, Jacque was in the midst of deep spiritual battle, and she felt lots of peace the night Evelyn prayed. The story continues that, another night, Evelyn ran out of gas on the highway and prayed for the Lord's protection as she was alone. A police officer stopped to help her, and he told Evelyn that he had just responded to a wreck that should have been fatal but which everyone survived. Still shaken, he asked if Evelyn believed in God, and she got to share about her faith. Know who was praying for her that night? Jacque![3] The Lord is intertwining our stories in such beautiful ways, making it possible to see Kingdom work that we would otherwise miss if we neglect his promptings to pray.

I decided that the next time I woke up in the middle of the night, I'd pray for the person whose name came to mind. Within days, I woke up at 3 a.m. with my heart beating rapidly. A first and last name came to mind, and I knew I should pray. Even in my half-awake state, I knew this had to be from God because it wasn't a person I knew or a familiar name—in fact, I didn't even know the last name *was* a last name. I told myself I'd remember the name and Google it in the morning, but as I started to wake, I could only remember a few letters.

My husband's faith is concrete and normally less emotional than mine. Even as I told him the story, I felt that if I remembered a name and was able to produce a Google search to show it was a real person, I could prove I wasn't over-sensationalizing this. But even without those facts, my sweet husband was quick to say that God had used me, and maybe I wasn't supposed to know the rest of the story.

We often expect to see the results of our prayers. We hear people experiencing amazing answered prayers and wish ours were that concrete too. But not understanding why we were prompted to pray shouldn't steal our joy or the privilege of getting to be a part of God's stories. Fighting the battle of spiritual warfare isn't just for ourselves. God can use you in the life of someone across the world with a name you can't even pronounce.

Get available for God. Let him know that you want to be a part of the work, and practice obedience when he calls.

How often would we find ourselves in prayer if we saw the spiritual realm more clearly? I'm convinced that the more we pray, the more we will desire to pray. So keep praying. Keep fighting. Remember it's not your battle. And remember to put on the right equipment. God gave us everything we need. Most of all, himself.

When we throw off the weight of sideshows and focus on the real battle, we can see God work in dramatic ways.

pray confidently & consistently

reflect

What human weapons have you tried to use in the past in spiritual warfare?

In what ways do Christians blend into the world so much that the devil doesn't even realize we're on the other side?

What spiritual battles faced by family members or friends could you intercede about?

read

- O 2 Corinthians 10:4
- O 1 Timothy 2:1
- O James 4:7

- O Exodus 14:14
- O 2 Chronicles 20:15

throwing off the weights that keep us
from praying consistently

12

Can I Get a Little Help?

Embracing Tools That Clear the Noise

HAVE YOU EVER PAINTED a picture of prayer that's more whimsical than the reality you experience every day? I've read books by prayer giants from previous centuries, and somehow it seems romantic when they stay up all night praying. Martin Luther is reported to have said, "I have so much to do today that I shall spend the first three hours in prayer."

Doesn't their world seem a bit idealized? Surely their lives were different than ours, and a thriving prayer life is just impossible in our world of school drop-offs and punching in with virtual time clocks. Prayer warriors of old didn't have screens to distract them or twenty-four-hour news or unlimited articles to fall down a rabbit hole reading.

Do the ideas in the following quote sound familiar? "This is not a praying age; it is an age of great activity, of great movements, but one in which the tendency is very strong to stress the seen and the material and to neglect and discount the unseen and the spiritual."[1] Is this not exactly how we feel in our world today—that everything is clamoring for our attention and we can't focus on the spiritual? Perhaps focused prayer is just too hard these days.

But here is an interesting fact. That quote above was written by E. M. Bounds . . . before 1914.

This is the reality: Every age has its own distractions and noise. And those who pray in each age need to find tools and methods to help them stay focused and dedicated.

In 2013, Val Marie Paper was a humble design company creating wedding invitations—and, looking back, not really great ones. As I balanced creating invitations and RSVP cards for couples' special days, I was also just trying to keep down my lunch in my first trimester of pregnancy. I am not a great pregnant lady. Some women glow. I have one friend who would gladly be a surrogate because she loves being pregnant so much. Me? I'll pass.

I'm a self-diagnosed hypochondriac, and I'm convinced I have the most sensitive nerves in the world. I *feel* everything! And pregnancy will give you no shortage of new things to feel in your body. I was desperate—and that's the way most good stories of prayer start.

I wanted to pray. I wanted to surrender so many things to the Lord: the sleep I feared missing, the closeness with my husband that I worried was in jeopardy, worries about being able to nurse without cursing, my desire for peace as a new mom, good communication between Tyler and me. And that was just for me! In that season, I also had several other pregnant friends and still more trying to conceive. So many things to pray about . . . I was overwhelmed.

Maybe you've experienced so many distractions that your thoughts fly all around the room. Maybe you've experienced the flustered, nothing's-coming-out feeling when you sit down to pray. How do we even begin when everything feels so urgent?

It was during this time that I dreamed up a journal format I was sure had to already exist. After two months of failed Google searches for said format, I gave up and created my own prayer journal. It was a place I could write down in neat little categories all the things I wanted to bring to the Lord each month. There was a section for personal prayer requests but also space for requests for the world, friends, family, and more. No more staring at the ceiling trying to figure out where to start. Time was a-wasting, and as pregnancy went on, the list of things I needed to surrender was piling up.

I spent months referencing my list related to sleep, breastfeeding, energy, and joy even in the notorious first six weeks after delivery. I also prayed for a safe delivery. In the years since then, I've reflected back on that journal that held so many fears and unknowns and that helped me see just how faithful God is.

One specific memory I have of God's faithfulness was Vivi's actual birth. Nine days before my due date, Vivi flipped to a breech position, making a C-section our most likely delivery option. A few weeks before finding that out, I had told Tyler I wanted to make a playlist for labor and delivery and really wanted Matt Maher's song "Lord, I Need You." The line "every hour I need you" spoke so strongly to me as I imagined hours of labor.[2] But after we shifted to preparing for a C-section birth, I forgot about the playlist.

On delivery day, as the nurses prepped me for surgery, I

was a mess. Major surgery was not in my birth plan. I asked the doctor if I could have music and he said yes, so my sister pulled out her phone and started a random worship playlist. As the anesthesiologist gave me my epidural, "Lord, I Need You" started playing. I was overcome by a peace I could never have mustered up on my own, and I felt joy as we welcomed our daughter into the world. The Lord showed up in such specific ways.

Even with amazing experiences like this, sometimes writing down our specific prayer requests can feel like cheating, no? Shouldn't we be able to pray big bold prayers without looking at what seems like a script? This was the lie that, had I not been so darn desperate, I would have believed. And I would have missed out on more joy and peace in that season than I ever thought possible.

This is the weight of self-sufficiency.

We miss out on a more vibrant prayer life when the enemy convinces us we should be able to focus on our own.

I was so desperate to bring my requests to the Lord despite pregnancy brain that I didn't give structure a second dirty look. I dove into it. Some may call it a crutch, but I saw it as a lifeline to the Lord.

My prayer journal was instrumental in helping me find focus in prayer. Prayer journals have become the central products of Val Marie Paper now, but at the time, I wasn't trying to start a business. I didn't even know that anyone else struggled to focus in prayer. Silly, right? I thought I must be the only flawed believer who spent most of my prayer time planning the day's tasks or, worse, shifting to worry that made me feel antsier than I had before I started praying.

If you've seen veteran pray-ers in action, you might feel

like your struggle to focus is unique to you and that you should have it all together. As I picture the lives of prayer warriors of old, I make a dangerous assumption that they didn't use tools or methods of prayer to help them stay focused. This assumption leaves me to flounder and say no to tools I fear I shouldn't need.

Can I share some tough love that I hope leaves you feeling comforted? You aren't God. You are made in his image, but you have limits. Those old prayer warriors you've seen in action or merely read about? They had limits too.

Even the disciples couldn't stay awake with Jesus. Matthew 26:40-41 says, "He came to the disciples [in the Garden of Gethsemane] and found them sleeping. And he said to Peter, 'So, could you not watch with me one hour? Watch and pray that you may not enter into temptation. The spirit indeed is willing, but the flesh is weak.'"

Weakness doesn't prove that you don't love God enough to focus perfectly. It proves you're human. It also proves that your enemy is at work to keep you from praying. Know what that means? It must be worth it!

So, friend, let's find the tools. Let's utilize the techniques that will keep bringing us back to God in prayer. They aren't evidence that we are too weak to become people of prayer. There's no such thing as too weak (see 2 Corinthians 12:10). Every weakness we have can either draw us closer to the Lord or point us away if pride takes over.

Even as I was writing this chapter, I got up from my computer and took a quick walk outside. I typically use these breaks to pray, and today, as I let the sun warm my bones, which were chilled from the coffee shop air conditioning, I prayed that the Lord would fill me with creativity and focus.

Tools over the years

For centuries, people have been coming up with solutions to help them pray without losing their focus.

- Susanna Wesley, mother of evangelists Charles and John Wesley, draped her apron over her head to pray in the midst of a noisy life with nineteen kids. The apron signaled to her children that Momma was praying!

- As a child, Amy Carmichael, who later became a missionary to India, would smooth her sheet on her bed and say to God, "Please come and sit with me."

- Preacher George Whitefield asked himself multiple questions each day, including these about his prayer life: "Have I been fervent in private prayer? Have I used stated hours of prayer? Have I used short communicative prayers every hour?"[3]

- When author Jill Briscoe sat in her kids' playpen, they knew it was mom's time in prayer.

- George Mueller would talk with God about what he'd studied in the Bible to get focused.

- Author Jeanne Guyon would read from a book of written prayers but made a point to stop reading when the Holy Spirit prompted her with her own words.

- James Gilmour, a nineteenth-century Scottish missionary to China, often wouldn't use a blotter on the wet ink when he was writing and reached the bottom of a page. Instead, he would wait until the ink dried and spend the time in prayer.

- Author Dick Eastman created a format of twelve areas to cover in hour-long prayer sessions, including confession, waiting, and Scripture-focused prayer.

- Paul E. Miller, author of *A Praying Life*, organized his prayers by creating index cards for each person or topic he wanted to pray about.

I prayed that he'd help me only share words that were his and not add my own untrue take on the Bible. I can't do it without him, so I pray for his presence and words to fill me. But you know what else I do as I write? I don't accept the distractions and assume that God will speak more loudly than the couple on their first date sitting near me. I utilize something called the Pomodoro method (periods of focused work followed by short breaks) because moving my body periodically means I don't destroy my back from poor posture. I play classical music or ocean sounds in my earbuds to drown out the oddly chosen coffee shop rock playlist.[*] I take timely breaks to ask the Lord to keep filling me up, and I'm grateful God has given me such practical tools.

Have you taken time to figure out any methods of prayer that work for you? Maybe it's a way to keep track of your prayer requests like index cards, a phone app, or one of our prayer journals. Maybe it's a loose format for daily prayer, a list of Scripture passages that help you focus your prayers, or a podcast that guides you through a prayer time. Search books, articles, or even Pinterest for ideas. In addition, take a look at the practical tips we've included throughout this book.

---

[*] You'd be flabbergasted by how much of this book was written with "If You Like Pina Coladas" or Journey drowned out in the background.

In this chapter, I want to share a few broad tools for your prayer life that I truly believe can help us throw off the weight of self-sufficiency. These techniques may look like crutches, but I don't think we need to be afraid of them if they help us find focus instead of bending to distraction.

Repetitious Prayers

According to many in our prayer community, one of the most common fears concerning prayer seems to be based on the New King James translation of Matthew 6:7, which refers to "vain repetitions": "When you pray, do not use vain repetitions as the heathen do. For they think that they will be heard for their many words."

Other translations use "empty phrases" (ESV), "babble"/ "babbling" (NLT, NIV), and "thoughtless repetition" (NASB). We talked about this briefly in chapter 2, but ultimately, this is referring to the way people from pagan religions would repeat formulas or certain words to seek the attention of their false gods. They thought if they said the right words in the right order enough times, the gods would see their devotion and would have to grant their request.

Some people have taken Jesus' admonition to mean that we shouldn't pray anything more than once. But does "vain repetition" truly sound like what we're doing when we continue each week to pray for our pastors to be protected from the enemy's schemes or for our families to experience unity? Praying about a particular issue over and over again is something we're called to do. In Luke 18 Jesus shares a parable about a persistent widow and prefaces it by explaining its meaning: Keep praying and don't give up. And if that weren't enough, he also put it into action as he awaited the Cross the night before in the Garden of Gethsemane. "So, leaving [the disciples] again, he went away and prayed for the third time, saying the same words again" (Matthew 26:44). Repetition in prayer reveals our faith in the Lord's ability to work even when we don't see an immediate result.

And what happens on a neural level as we pray something over and over again is amazing. Neural pathways create what we can picture as grooves in our brains, and those grooves get deeper the more we think a particular thought. This is great for positive thoughts, but unfortunately, it's also true for negative thoughts.

The good news? God has designed us with the ability to rewrite these thoughts. Romans 12:2 calls us to "not be conformed to this world, but be transformed by the renewal of your mind." Isaiah 26:3 promises peace for those "whose mind is stayed on" God. Second Corinthians 10:5 tells us to "destroy arguments and every lofty opinion raised against the knowledge of God, and take every thought captive to obey Christ." We have power to use our minds in ways that will transform us, bring us peace, and free us from the lies of the enemy. That's great news! The reality, though, is that I don't do this enough.

I want new grooves. I want a new pattern of thinking, of surrender, of faith. And oddly enough, repetition in prayer doesn't stand in the way of that. In fact, repetition can actually help increase it. As we pray for something repeatedly, we're creating deeper grooves in our brains and a more God-honoring thought pattern about that thing.

David created new grooves in Psalm 56. Verse 4 says, "In God, whose word I praise—in God I trust and am not afraid. What can mere mortals do to me?" (NIV). Then verses 10-11 use some of the same language: "In God, whose word

I praise, in the LORD, whose word I praise—in God I trust and am not afraid. What can man do to me?" (NIV).

In between these lines, David is rehashing with God all the ways his enemies are coming after him. Then it's as if he realizes the way out of his worries is to remember the very truth he just spoke in verse 4. In fact, before he repeats the line he says, "This I know, that God is for me" (verse 9). He's reminding himself of what he knows to be true.

When seeing a whole line repeated in a Scripture passage, I used to be tempted to think there was some sort of error. Now I think about how these Bible characters aren't "characters" at all but real people who needed to rewrite their thoughts too.

Are you praying for the Lord to bring your husband to salvation? For a wayward child to find his faith? For a job that will utilize your gifts? For deep friendships? Imagine lifting that up repeatedly to the Lord and consistently surrendering it to him.

Prayer is not simply talking to God about your problem. It's an act of surrender. In Luke 9:23, Jesus calls us to take up our cross daily: "If any of you wants to be my follower, you must give up your own way, take up your cross daily, and follow me" (NLT). Doesn't it make sense that we will need to lay things down more than once too?

I don't think we have an inkling how powerful it is to keep coming back to God about the same concerns. What might look to us like a lack of faith on our part (badgering a God who's obviously forgotten us) is actually strengthening the grooves of surrender and faith.

I've been learning in a fresh way lately about praying consistently for things far in the future, and I've been excited to do it. In fact, sweet reader, I've been praying for you for more than fifteen months. This book is set to release in the fall of 2021, and in May of 2020, I started praying daily for the impact this book would have and for every person who would read it. If you read this years after publication, phew—you have been sufficiently covered, my friend.

I get misty-eyed picturing you reading those words over *you* right now, and I pray you feel loved. Not just by a human like me but by your Creator, who is repeatedly prompting the hearts of some of his kids to pray for some of his other kids. What love from a Father to keep prompting hearts for *me* and for *you*.

Selah.

Hard stop. We need to pause here. Did you catch the beauty of God's love for us in repetition? He keeps chasing our hearts and loving us through other believers over and over again. Repetition can be beautiful when we see it first through the Father's love. Imagine getting to reflect back a loving repetition to the Father.

We don't repeat areas of prayer because we're somehow "doing it wrong." We don't write down the same requests month after month because we failed the first time. We do it as an act of worship. We tell God, "I know you're still God, so I'm still giving this to you."

That's pretty much the opposite of dull, if you ask me.

Written Prayers

A friend introduced me to the book *Every Moment Holy* by Douglas Kaine McKelvey, which is a book of beautifully written prayers for different occasions. Some prayers were for everyday occasions, like waking up or going to bed, while others were for specific occasions, like the first hearth fire of the season or changing diapers. I loved thumbing through the book and expanding my ideas of things to pray for. Somehow I had totally missed the books of prayers others had long loved, such as *The Valley of Vision* (a book of Puritan prayers) or the liturgical books of prayers my Catholic friends grew up reading. This was all new to me.

> Maybe the reason prayer feels boring sometimes is because we've only used the words we already know to say.

After I shared many of my own written prayers with my online community, readers began requesting that I compile my own book of prayers. To be honest, I was hesitant. I didn't want my words to be a substitute for what someone else would communicate to the Father. It was my passion to help women grow their prayer lives, and I worried I'd be introducing a speed bump into their conversations. What I realized from my own experience reading written prayers, though, is that they acted more like bumpers on a bowling lane than like bumps in the road. Others' words didn't slow me down but, instead, helped shape my own prayers and kept me from going off track.[*]

I think my fears were valid. We *can* depend on the words of others too much. But if we let the fear of using written prayers paralyze us, we shortchange our prayer lives. Maybe the reason prayer feels boring sometimes is because we've only used the words we already know to say.

---

[*]In case you're wondering, I did write that book. I called it *Springboard Prayers* because I wanted to emphasize how written prayers could be the jumping-off point for readers to continue to talk to God on their own. I included questions and prompts to help keep the conversation going.

tip ————————————————————————————————

Here are some categories I encourage users of our prayer journals to pray over each month, along with some specific requests in those categories that we consistently lift up.

- Our world—the poor and needy, the global church
- Our nation—racial reconciliation, political leaders
- Our community—to be a light to our neighbors, local nonprofits
- Our churches—for the pastors and elders to stand against the enemy's attacks, kids' and youth ministry, unity
- Our loved ones—salvation, for gratitude and peace in our home, no sickness
- Our friends—growing friendships
- Personal requests—peace and joy in the Lord, wisdom and understanding, passion for the Word and prayer

How amazing is it that we can read words of other prayers, words that we would never instinctively think of on our own and also wouldn't be able to fathom because our faith isn't big enough yet? Think about reading Jesus' prayer in the Garden of Gethsemane. I've already mentioned how his words "Not my will but yours be done" hold so much power because I want to say them with confidence. But truth be told, they wouldn't naturally flow from my human heart had I not read Jesus saying them. Reading prayers from other believers can shift so much in our hearts. It can add a depth and breadth to our prayers that goes way beyond the few things we normally pray about and the shallower way we ask for them.

Give it a try! If you're looking for words from Scripture to pray, Psalm 23 is a great place to start. Also, at the end of the book, I've included a brief prayer for each weight we're trying to throw off as we pursue a deeper prayer life. And if you're still wondering whether it's possible to read someone else's words, even multiple times, and get anything out of it, think of worship music. Have you listened to a song dozens of times that still makes you tear up or causes you to lift your hands to the sky? If we're okay singing the same worship songs over and over again to express praise, I think we can embrace written prayers without fear.

Designated Prayer Times

As I was simultaneously reading Daniel and Acts recently, I noticed that both books referenced people praying at certain times of day. I started digging into this idea of having designated prayer times.

- Daniel prayed three times a day (Daniel 6:10).
- Peter and John went to the temple at "the ninth hour" to pray (Acts 3:1).
- Peter prayed at "the sixth hour" (Acts 10:9).
- Cornelius prayed at "the ninth hour" (Acts 10:30).

According to the Jewish calendar, these were the fixed hours of prayer mentioned in the Bible: the third hour (approximately 9 a.m.), the sixth hour (12 p.m.), and the ninth hour (3 p.m.). At these times, devout men in Jerusalem would go to the Temple to pray, while Israelites who were exiled to other countries, like Daniel, would open their windows and face Jerusalem while they prayed.

I'll admit, my greatest takeaway from designated prayer times has nothing to do with ancient practices. It's just a super practical reminder to pray throughout the day. Having a set time to pray doesn't have to steal the romance. It can enhance it, just as repetition doesn't have to dull our faith but can increase it.

It's easy to see our prayer lives the way we see romance through the eyes of a rom-com. We have an expectation that romance will be a series of impromptu run-ins where everything eventually falls into place. My favorite rom-com is *When Harry Met Sally*. As a former journalist myself who hoped to marry her best friend, it checked all the right boxes. Every five years or so, the protagonists ran into each other, and after several of these chance encounters, they eventually fell in love. Can you imagine if the storyline were that every few years they would meet, check their calendars, and pencil in their next rendezvous for five years down the road? Where's the fun in that?

We love the rush of an unexpected rendezvous that changes our lives, and I think we expect the same of our relationship with God. We think we should only pray when we want to. Otherwise, aren't we just kind of faking it? I really don't think so.

A mom still has to change diapers even though she doesn't love to do it.

A writer still has to write to make a deadline, even if he or she doesn't feel like it.

A good athlete finishes the game or the race, even when there's no longer a chance of winning.

And if anything, when we stick to something after the honeymoon phase wears off, we are deepening our affections. We are no longer choosing it just because it makes us feel good. We are acting out of faithfulness and commitment.

Based on the conversations I've had with hungry prayers over the years, people's greatest desire is to learn how to discern God's voice. I fear we're not hearing him speak to us because we're waiting for his voice to fall on us like manna from the sky when he really told us to gather the grain and bake the bread ourselves. The best way to hear from God is to regularly listen to God.

I love what happens to Cornelius in Acts 10:2-3. He was "a devout man who feared God with all his household, gave alms generously to the people, and prayed continually to God. About the ninth hour of the day he saw clearly in a vision an angel of God come in and say to him, 'Cornelius.'" The ninth hour was most likely during his regularly scheduled prayer time. It was likely the time the Lord knew Cornelius would have open ears and an open heart. And what a coincidence that this was the moment he saw a vision of an angel. Here's what happened next.

> And [the angel] said to him, "Your prayers and your alms have ascended as a memorial before God. And now send men to Joppa and bring one Simon who is called Peter. He is lodging with one Simon, a tanner, whose house is by the sea." When the angel who spoke to him had departed, he called two of his servants and a devout soldier from among those who attended him, and having related everything to them, he sent them to Joppa.
> ACTS 10:4-8

So the sequence of events was this: 1) Cornelius prayed, 2) he heard God's command, and 3) he obeyed. I'm convinced all three of these are tied together instead of the vision being some serendipitous moment. I'm convinced that Cornelius's obedience was influenced by this regular time of prayer. I'm convinced because I see in my own life that my heart is ripe to obey when I'm bowed low in prayer before the Lord. When I'm running around, I've got better excuses for not listening. The phrase "on the go" implies I'm already heading in one direction, and obedience requires that I slow down and consider going a different way.

> Having fixed, consistent times with the Lord means I am creating a healthy rhythm of listening in my life.

God can grab hold of our hearts anywhere and anytime, but I'm learning that having fixed, consistent times with the Lord means I am creating a healthy rhythm of listening in my life. It's not a burden to check off a list but an ongoing proclamation to the Lord that I am his vessel, ready to be poured into. If we feel like God's gone quiet on us, if we're waiting for that serendipitous run-in with our heavenly Father, can we shift our expectations and commit to meeting with him faithfully and regularly? Can we make a practical change and clear even five minutes from the midst of a busy schedule to reorient our hearts toward God with praise and listening? It feels like such a small thing, but we see God repeatedly use these moments in our lives.

I've heard moms say that one of the best things they did as their kids grew up was to have regular times where they were available. Sometimes that meant asking questions, but more often than not, it simply meant consistent moments of being in a nearby room, not on the phone but ready and willing if their kids needed to talk. Not every day produced earth-shattering conversations, but the commitment and loyalty the moms showed meant that when the children did need something, they had no doubt they could find their mom available and ready to listen.

I can see how consistent time makes sense with God, too—not because he's waiting to cry to us about how a kid at school wasn't nice but because he's looking for willing hearts. That regular time can feel like a waste when nothing big seems to happen, but we have no idea what it reveals to the Lord about our devotion to him. God's not looking for the strongest or brightest. He's looking for those willing to be used by him. And coming consistently to the throne room lets him know we are open for any assignment he has to give us.

When We Just Don't Wanna

What about those moments when we just don't want to pray? I honestly don't think we feel that way because we're too busy or because prayer's too boring. I think it's because the idea of choosing prayer in a noisy world is the equivalent of this sweets-lover choosing a natural strawberry over a bowl of ice cream.

Highly processed sugar is the easy choice and will always be waiting to tempt us. Fruit, though satisfying, has fewer chemically addictive qualities than ice cream. So if we don't get intentional and actively pursue prayer, we will drift to the ultra-sweet stuff of distractions instead of the satisfying fruit that awaits us.

- The world offers seemingly immediate results, while prayer requires patience.
- The world offers stimulation at lightning speed, while prayer requires that we sit and learn to embrace the quiet needed for listening.

- The world offers mind-numbing entertainment, while prayer requires our minds.

One of my favorite inside jokes with my husband is from a video montage of parents telling their kids that they ate the kids' Halloween candy. For just a minute, forget the fact that parents are straight up lying to their kids and kids are flipping out about candy. The part that made us laugh was when one kid matter-of-factly told his mom, "You're probably gonna get a bellyache." Now Tyler and I throw this phrase around when we indulge in those things that never feel good afterward.

The distractions won't satisfy. They're too sweet, and you're probably gonna get a bellyache. Grab the natural, sweet, delicious strawberry. Shut off the TV. Turn off the podcasts in the car. Stop listening to the voice messages from friends when you cook. Instead, pray. It's sweet, and it won't leave you with a bellyache.

I cannot tell you how many times I've tried to escape prayer by choosing other things, only to finally pray and wish

tip ────────────────────────────

Think about your schedule, and come up with some regular times when you can pause and pray each day. A few ideas:

- Getting ready for the day
- Driving to school or work
- Taking the dog for a walk
- Mealtimes
- Those few minutes before you pick up kids from school or activities

I had come sooner. The temptation to face distraction on our own is real. But when we fall for the lie that we should be able to have these burning-bush conversations on the fly or in the midst of constant noise, it's like me convincing myself I should have enough self-control to always choose the strawberries over the ice cream. We fool ourselves and are left disappointed with a lackluster prayer life.

Let repetition, written prayers, or designated prayer times deepen your love and commitment into something that lasts longer than your favorite rom-com. When we throw off the weight of self-sufficiency and admit we need help with our prayer lives, we'll find tools that will strengthen our relationship with God.

reflect

What subconscious expectations have you placed on yourself to focus during prayer in your own strength?

What's your most common reason for not praying, and how can you take action on it?

Are there any resources or methods to try that could help you foster a deeper prayer life?

read

- ○ 1 Thessalonians 5:16-18
- ○ Psalm 119:148
- ○ Philippians 4:8
- ○ Psalm 92:1-2

13

Did You Want to Say Something?

Quieting My Own Voice to Hear His

I'VE BEEN ASKING too many questions since the day I picked up a steno pad and interviewed my first "source" in college. As a journalism major, I learned the art of asking questions to find out information. One technique was to ask similar questions in different ways, allowing a source to expand on a thought. Then there was the silver bullet of not filling every pause but giving my interviewee plenty of space to respond. Outside of news reporting, my skill in question asking has gotten me in trouble many times at social events—or, at the very least, caused my husband a little embarrassment as I asked things the average human wouldn't unless they were conducting a job interview.

But there's one person in my life I don't ask a lot of questions. Instead, I talk and request stuff and talk some more and then hop up as soon as I'm done talking because I assume that's the end of the conversation. Unfortunately, this just so happens to be the most important conversation I get to partake in.

This is the weight of monologuing.

We miss out on half the conversation of prayer if we do all the talking.

For many of us, this is what our current prayer lives look like. We're unsure what everyone else is talking about when they say prayer is powerful and fascinating and that God meets them there and speaks. We feel like we're just running through our list of grievances only to get up at the end of our prayer time and feel exactly the same as we did when we started.

Picture it with me. Two people are in a conversation together. One is babbling on about trivial things, believing they are quite earth-shattering, while the other holds his tongue waiting to say something that's *actually* earth-shattering. He doesn't interrupt but patiently waits for an opening when the other person will stop talking. And that moment never comes. The chatty person says her piece and walks off.

No dialogue. No *aha* moments. No comfort. No challenging insights. No interaction. Just one big monologue.

This is not a conversation I'd remember much. And this isn't the path to a thriving prayer life. This isn't the avenue to daily moments of hearing God. God is not silent. If anything, we attempt to silence him in a thousand unintentional ways.

I'm not suggesting that God doesn't care about the smallest things in our lives. Quite the contrary. And I think if we remembered how genuinely he cares for us and what his presence means for us, we'd make more room for him to speak.

We might even cut our own stories short in hopes of getting to the really good stuff he wants to tell us.

We assume the good stuff is our list we're desperate to share with the Lord. But when I remember that the Creator of the universe actually wants to speak to me, I should probably assume that what he's got to say in a conversation will be monumental. He doesn't want to talk just because he enjoys the sound of his own voice as many of us humans do. He speaks with intention and purpose. Proverbs 2:6 says, "For the LORD gives wisdom; from his mouth come knowledge and understanding."

I'll be honest—it's not lost on me that God gives wisdom. I know he has good things to tell me. And of course I want his divine opinion on everything; I just didn't know it was necessary to ask for it. But it is. Not because God is a pouty God who wants to be asked or else his feelings will get hurt but because, if I'm not asking, it's hard for me to tune into the answers. What answers would I even know to look for? When we practice the art of having an actual conversation with God, we're inviting his response and priming ourselves to hear it.

The weight holding you back from a thriving prayer life may feel like a God not willing to speak, but I promise that's not it. Instead, there's a chance we're expecting him to interrupt us if he's got something to say, and we immediately leave the conversation if he takes too long to respond.

When God Speaks

Lately I've been feeling like I cannot make a decision to save my life.

I am usually a super decisive person. My spiritual gift is discernment. I've got right and wrong pegged pretty accurately. I know what I like, and I know what I don't like. Wishy-washy is never how I'd describe myself. Opinionated? Yes. Too opinionated? I can't deny it.

Over the last few months, I've been overloaded with intense mental stress that led to lots of mistakes and no small amount of guilt. The first thing to break was my ability to make decisions. I've felt unsure of every decision, big or small, from the weighty choices to minor things like which shirt I should wear today.

This morning, Val Marie Paper launched our annual collection of products, and I was feeling nostalgic for the coffee shop where I normally posted on launch days. I couldn't sit inside due to COVID-19 restrictions, but I decided to park outside and take a little walk as I typically enjoy doing before I start my workdays. The quick seven-minute loop affords me a chance to pray and surrender to the Lord the work I'm about to do. Today, I listened to a quick audio snippet from a pastor who encouraged his listeners to ask God for the guidance we needed. So I did. It was almost too easy.

Over the next thirty minutes, as I finished my walk and drove home, I simply made space to think. I grieved. I begged. I pondered. I talked out my concerns as you would with a counselor. And you know how a good counselor gives you the space to think about something you normally wouldn't make time for? Somehow revelations come without a word, but you know that if you hadn't been in his or her presence, it never would have happened in the hustle and bustle of life.

Well, God's power and presence are on another level than a counselor's—obviously—but sometimes the results are similar. Listening isn't always about what God will speak back. Many times, it's being still in his presence that brings the greatest transformation. We see this in several places in Scripture:

> Come to me, all who labor and are heavy laden, and
> I will give you rest. Take my yoke upon you, and
> learn from me, for I am gentle and lowly in heart,
> and you will find rest for your souls. For my yoke is
> easy, and my burden is light.
> MATTHEW 11:28-30

It's not the doing but the receiving of his yoke that brings relief.

> We all, with unveiled face, beholding the glory of
> the Lord, are being transformed into the same image
> from one degree of glory to another.
> 2 CORINTHIANS 3:18

It's not the doing but the beholding of the Lord that transforms us.

> Don't copy the behavior and customs of this world,
> but let God transform you into a new person by
> changing the way you think. Then you will learn to
> know God's will for you, which is good and pleasing
> and perfect.
> ROMANS 12:2, NLT

It's not in our doing but in our thinking that we are changed.

This morning, the truth God reminded me of cleared my mentally exhausted brain, filled me with joy I hadn't experienced in months, and grounded me in a patience my girls hadn't experienced in a while.

I believe God shows us more than we think he does. Sure, we're not going to see his whole plan, but I get glimpses when I open my eyes to them. I'm not walking around all ears to God 24-7, with him deciding to grace me with his presence only every now and then. It's actually the reverse. God is always in the conversation, and I remember to pop in only when things get hard or I'm facing a choice and have no clue what to do.

The Lord adamantly wants us to know he speaks. Why do we struggle to hear him? I was struck by this quote: "I don't think we realize how much our use of technology and its assault on our attention has made this difficult to do. You can't give God your attention when your attention is constantly being targeted and taken captive . . . and you're cooperating."[1]

The last few months have had me buzzing around from flower to flower like a worker bee: no rest, no pauses. At one point, I texted my sister late one night telling her I needed a pep talk. I couldn't get up from the couch where I was finishing a big project. I told her that I felt like I couldn't stop moving. If I did, I'd die—like a shark that stops swimming. It wasn't true, but it's what I'd convinced myself of. And you better believe it stole my focus.

The things targeting your attention, the things taking you captive, are trying to convince you that they matter most. What lie is keeping you too busy to hear God?

Selah.

Each December, I choose a word or phrase I want to focus on in the year ahead. In 2020, my phrase was "Make Room" because I wanted to make more room for God. Ironically, I spent February to September thinking I could do that without actually making room. I tried to squeeze God into what little space I could find, but I never cleared out room for him. And as the God of the universe, he's worthy of me clearing out space for him.

Maybe you need this reminder today too. God is all ears. Give him the floor for a few minutes, and I pray you find yourself cross-legged in awe as you hear him speak.

We Can't Miss Out

If you were a journalist, who's the person you'd most want to interview? Who's the person you could easily ask a thousand questions and still hang on their every word? Maybe you'd even go home and reread your notes again and again just to replay what happened and make sure you didn't miss any goodness.

This is the opportunity we have with the Creator of the universe. The God who made us, loves us, and has the best plan for us is telling us to come to him for knowledge and wisdom. We've been given the opportunity to ask God questions in prayer, yet all too often, we're the ones who take the mic the entire time.

We're all so desperate for clarity. And while clarity may not come every time we ask, if it does come, it will be because God is illuminating truth that he wants us to know. Jeremiah 33:3 says, "Call to me and I will answer you, and will tell you great and hidden things that you have not known."

If the words that God longs to share with us are of any value, we need to remove the weight of monologuing from our conversations. We need to figure out on a practical level what it means to listen to God. We need to develop a fear of missing out on conversations with the Creator of the universe that's greater than our fear of missing out on the latest news story, neighborhood gossip, or iPhone model.

Missing time with God feels like missing a vacuum. Skipping an episode of my favorite new reality show or losing the chance to hear the latest installment of work drama from my friend feels like missing something I *need* to know. But not hearing God speak? I don't even know what I'm missing. I have a world of distractions beckoning me, and I cooperate.

So how do we un-cooperate with the world? How do we hear God in our noisy worlds?

1. Get Expectant

First and foremost, we must remember that God longs to speak to us. If we don't know that, why would we get expectant?

You might be asking, "What does it actually mean to be *expectant*?" Oxford Dictionary defines it as "having or showing an excited feeling that something is about to happen, especially something pleasant and interesting."[2]

Can you imagine if we brought that energy to our prayers? If we waited with an excited feeling for the Lord to speak? If we knew something was "about to happen"? I want to be expectant. I want to pray and be so sure God is going to respond that I'm on the lookout for his response. I've got pen and paper ready to jot down his thoughts. I don't walk off and say, "He can call me if he gets the message."

We're not leaving voicemails. We're in a conversation.

To really live expectantly, we might need to dive into

God's Word and hunker down on his promises that he hears us and responds. We may need to read through Scripture and recognize each and every time someone cries out to God and he answers. Isaac. Moses. Hannah. Samuel. David. Paul. Cornelius. It's truly overwhelming.

We may need to ask more questions and maintain a posture of waiting for a response, especially in those seasons that we know hold little quiet. A few years ago, when my youngest daughter was born, I made something called "Expectant Cards." With a newborn, my quiet times were few and far between, and I wanted a way to connect with God in the middle of my days. I wanted a way to look and listen for God no matter how little time I could set aside.

My "Expectant Cards" had a Bible verse on one side along with some notes on the back about different words that stood out when I'd read the verse in a few different translations. Each card also included a question I wanted to ask God. One card included James 5:7-8, and I asked God, "What does it mean to establish my heart?" After I read Zechariah 4:10, I asked God to show me what work he was just beginning that I could rejoice in.

When you end prayer time with a question, it's implied that the conversation is continuing. Just because you get up doesn't mean the conversation is over. When we ask a friend a question, we don't immediately turn around and walk off. Our ears are wide open, and we are ready to listen. Reviewing the Scripture on these cards and thinking about a question was my way of getting my heart in a listening posture for the day.

Whether or not you make your own "Expectant Cards," you can find a way to come before God each day with a heart that's ready to listen and expecting him to respond.

2. Make Room

If we've let our worlds become wall-to-wall noise, we're implying either that God isn't going to speak to us or that he's going to barge in like the Kool-Aid Man when we yell, "Hey, God!" I've been the girl wondering why God ghosted me when my every car ride was filled with music, my every walk was filled with podcasts, and my every cleaning session was filled with TV. If this conversation is as vital as we say it is, we have to make room for God to speak.

My husband has mastered this technique when we're out and he runs into a friend. I giggle every time it happens. Inevitably, a conversation ends—or that's what it looks like to me. But my husband and his friend awkwardly stand around for five painfully silent seconds only to pick the conversation back up. To me, the silence looked like an exit point. To them, it looked like a processing pause. Yes, it looks awkward, but what flows after the pause is beautiful. Neither one was looking for a quick exit.

> If this conversation is as vital as we say it is, we have to make room for God to speak.

Can we approach prayer similarly and not take the seemingly obvious end of the conversation to be the end? Can we embrace a little awkwardness and not turn tail and run when the silence gets uncomfortable?

If our comfort level is the main factor in how long we pray, we absolutely won't experience the fruit that's possible in our prayer lives. The good news is that making room for God doesn't require us to do more. It requires us to be okay with doing less—and to be okay with the awkwardness of silence or the itch we feel when we want to add noise to our day.

Our enemy wants to make us uncomfortable with silence because he knows how effective silence can be.

If you're like me, you feel soothed by noise. If I'm home alone, I might turn on the TV just to have a little noise. Quiet feels too quiet. And if I'm really honest, being alone with my thoughts can sometimes be scary, and I distract myself with noise and media so I have less time to think. But those distractions never do what I hope they will. There's a time and place for conversations and sermons or worship music in our earbuds, but even that can be us choosing what we think we need to hear or even what we think God wants to say to us rather than making space for God himself to speak.

Making room for God equals possibilities beyond our own expectations. Ephesians 3:20 says, "Now all glory to God, who is able, through his mighty power at work within us, to accomplish infinitely more than we might ask or think" (NLT). Make plenty of room for the Lord to come in, and, I promise you, he will.

It's in prayer that I most often see Jesus as the symbolic Lamb of God. He's not storming the gates of our minds and competing with all the things we distract ourselves with. He's patient, quiet, and humble. And goodness, aren't we grateful for that? He comes in a gentle wind (1 Kings 19:9-12). He invites us to rest (Matthew 11:28-30). He "makes me lie down in green pastures . . . leads me beside still waters . . . restores my soul" (Psalm 23:2-3).

Want to know the craziest thing? With more than seven billion people on the planet, God is still able to give each of us his undivided attention. God is not scanning a text message while we pray. He's sitting there fully listening and remembering every word. Can you even imagine the response we'll get to hear if we wait for him? No halfhearted comments like *Oh, that's great. Uh-huh. Sounds nice. You'll be fine.* True heart connection awaits.

3. Survey the Land

If we are looking for God to speak in one specific way, we'll likely think he's staying silent, and we will put off prayer. Instead of expecting a specific response, we must survey the land. We need to take time to look for God in all areas of life, not just the one area we're waiting for him to move in. Many times, where he is working is not the predictable spot we expect him to be.

> Where have we lost our hearing because we're expecting God to work only in one way?

In his book *A Gentle Thunder*, Max Lucado shares a story of a man who told God he would listen if God spoke to him in the powerful ways he had spoken to Moses, Joshua, and the disciples. God did speak—but in quiet ways, bringing down walls of sin and stilling internal storms. The story concludes:

> *But because the man was looking at bushes, not hearts; bricks and not lives, seas and not souls, he decided that God had done nothing.*
>
> *Finally he looked to God and asked, Have you lost your power? And God looked at him and said, Have you lost your hearing?*[3]

Where have we lost our hearing because we're expecting God to work only in one way? If you want a practical place to start when you're figuring out where to look for God, consider Charles Stanley's list of ways that God gets our attention:

- A restless spirit
- A word from others
- Blessings
- Unanswered prayer
- Disappointment
- Unusual circumstances
- Failure
- Financial collapse
- Tragedy
- Sickness and affliction[4]

Survey the land of your life. Where is God moving that you didn't expect? What have you chalked up to coincidence or something that "would have happened anyway" that might have been God speaking to you? What is God doing in one spot while you've had your eyes peeled in the other direction? What nuances are you seeing only because you're looking for them?

Pray. Ask God to show these things to you, and don't get up so fast that you miss them.

4. Recognize His Voice

Most importantly, as we listen for God, we need to know his voice. Perhaps one of the main reasons we don't feel like we hear God is that we don't know whether we are hearing him speaking to us or whether that's our own gut or our best friend.

God can speak through our circumstances and the people in our lives, but if we want to really recognize the voice of God, we must know what he has already written to us. Second Timothy 3:16-17 says, "All Scripture is breathed out by God and profitable for teaching, for reproof, for correction, and for training in righteousness, that the man of God may be complete, equipped for every good work." In his Word, we understand the heart and even the tone of God. This is why reading the Bible is so intertwined with our prayer lives. They aren't two separate entities. What we know from God's Word will play an enormous role in what we believe about God. So many times, though, we're not weighing one good option against an evil one. And that's where things feel tricky.

How do we learn to recognize God's voice?

- We get to know Scripture. God will not contradict what he's said in his Word.

- We remember who God is. His voice won't go against his nature (e.g., an unloving, berating voice is not from God).

- We pay attention to what's going on around us. God often confirms what he's saying through a repeated verse that keeps coming up, a sermon on the very topic you're struggling with, etc.

- We listen to wise counsel. God can speak to us through godly people in our lives.

- We obey when he speaks. Disobedience dulls our hearing. Obedience sharpens it.

On the cusp of COVID-19 changing our lives, our team at Val Marie Paper found ourselves getting ready for a big outdoor market. Each year we spend three solid days talking to and praying with customers and telling new people about our journals. It's one of my favorite things to do because I get to come face-to-face with our customers and hear how our journals have changed their prayer lives. Our team spends months preparing, and at the beginning of March, we spent an entire day setting up our booth.

The COVID-19 situation was changing fast, and throughout the day, news outlets were reporting cancellations of major events. As we headed to an informational meeting before the official kickoff the next day, the market's event team told the vendors they would have to officially cancel the event. Since we were already set up, though, they said we could stay if we felt comfortable. They'd need to know our decision before we left the building.

Our team found a quiet spot in the meeting room and plopped on the floor and prayed. We had no idea what to do. Should we stay and risk being in contact with thousands of people? Should we head home? Was the enemy trying to distract us from something big that would happen that weekend? We genuinely didn't know.

First we sat and prayed. Then we talked about the situation and shared our thoughts. It turned out that we all separately felt confident about staying. Then we prayed again, asking the Lord to make it abundantly clear whether we were making a decision outside his will.

Later that evening, we got the email: The city was revoking street permits. We needed to tear down the booth the next morning at 8 a.m., and then we would be going home.

As devastated as we were to hear this news, we were grateful for the clear direction we had prayed for just a few hours before. The answer wasn't what we'd hoped for, but we were able to rest in the fact that this was God's plan. I drove home, and the following day I got to attend Vana's school program, which I hadn't expected to do. A few short hours later, I was home to hear the news that my girls' school would be closing. We couldn't foresee how the coronavirus, social distancing, quarantine, or stay-at-home orders would become common terms just a few days later.

As I've said before, I'm so thankful the decisions I make don't rest on my own wisdom. And boy, was this another big reminder of that. But I was grateful that we had taken the time to listen to God and seek his leading. I'm glad he heard our cries for a clear answer that we could not miss. Times like these help us practice identifying his voice and remind us how important it is to make space for him.

tip ────────────────────────────────

When you're ready to deepen the conversation, consider asking God one of these questions during your prayer time:

- What good things have been idols distracting me from you?
- What victories have you given me that I need to rejoice in?
- Where do I need to obey today?
- Whom have you put in my path to serve today?
- What attitudes are you working to change in my heart?
- How can I honor you today with how I spend my time?
- How can I show your love to my family today?
- How should I be praying for _____?

Listening to God is a privilege. It's not something to bemoan or begrudgingly cram into our schedules. Listening allows us to be led by the one who created us. We're blessed that this is even possible. We didn't do one thing to deserve it.

Psalm 69:16 sums it up so beautifully: "Answer my prayers, O LORD, for your unfailing love is wonderful. Take care of me, for your mercy is so plentiful" (NLT). Answer me, O God, not because *I* am good but because *you* are. We are not entitled to the ear of God Almighty, but he is good and freely offers it to us. We'd be silly not to accept the gift of his attention and knowledge, right?

When we stop talking so much in prayer and throw off the weight of monologuing, we can be ready to hear all that the Lord wants to share with us.

reflect

What lie is keeping you too busy to hear God?

What would it look like to embrace some possibly awkward silence and keep prayer going beyond your own words?

What is God doing in one spot while you've had your eyes peeled in the other direction?

read

○ Jeremiah 33:3
○ Matthew 7:24

○ Psalm 32:8-9
○ Isaiah 30:21

14

Are You Sure That Command Was for Me?

Learning to Pair Prayer and Fasting

FASTING WAS SOMETHING I hadn't dug into much in all my years of pursuing prayer. I can't say for sure why, but it may have something to do with the fact that I'm not the type of girl who likes to skip a meal. I was content to leave fasting for situations like, say, receiving the Ten Commandments (Moses) or resisting the actual devil in the wilderness (Jesus). I'm just over here making journals and taking care of kids. What could a little lunch hurt?

This is the weight of comforts.

I miss out on spiritual breakthrough when I neglect pairing fasting with prayer.

If we want deeper prayer lives and the spiritual breakthrough we're not currently experiencing, there's a chance our comfort is standing in the way. This one is hard for me.

I love my comforts. If there's one thing I've taught my girls well, it's how to get cozy. If it's raining outside, Vivi suggests I park in the garage so we don't get wet, and we all enjoy huddling under blankets to watch a good movie. Vana is the cuddle queen. She prefers to say "comfy" instead of "cozy," and her pronunciation is one I hope I always remember.

I'm good at comfy, and skipping meals isn't comfy.

But know what? It's absolutely necessary and super rewarding.

Why Fast?

After doing a quick Google search of all the instances of fasting in Scripture and filling a yellow legal pad with a list of references, I opened my Bible and started reading.

And fun fact: Pretty much all the major players fasted. I was hard-pressed to find a favorite Bible character who *hadn't* fasted at one point or another. I knew fasting was a good thing to do, but seeing a lineup of those men and women in the Bible, who saw God work in incredible ways, commit to fasting? That was eye-opening.

Biblical fasters

Moses fasted for forty days and nights while writing down the Ten Commandments (Exodus 34).

Elijah fasted for forty days and nights before hearing God speak in a whisper (1 Kings 19).

King Darius fasted while he prayed for Daniel's protection in the lions' den (Daniel 6).

Daniel fasted as he pled for mercy from God for the Israelites' unfaithfulness (Daniel 9).

Daniel fasted in mourning for three weeks before receiving a vision (Daniel 10).

> *Daniel is kiiind of a legend when it comes to prayer and fasting.*

Nehemiah fasted for his people in the face of the destruction of Jerusalem's wall (Nehemiah 1).

Paul said he fasted often (2 Corinthians 11:27, KJV).

Need some women examples? I've got it.

Esther fasted before confronting her husband, King Xerxes, and saving the Jews (Esther 4).

The prophetess Anna consistently fasted in the Temple (Luke 2:36-38).

What about corporate fasting? Got that, too.

The Israelites, facing defeat in battle, fasted before a victory (Judges 20).

The Israelites fasted while they mourned the loss of King Saul and his son Jonathan (2 Samuel 1).

King Jehoshaphat proclaimed a fast for Judah in the face of danger from an enemy invasion (2 Chronicles 20).

Ezra proclaimed a fast to humble the people's hearts and pray for God's protection (Ezra 8).

The Ninevites fasted after recognizing their sinful ways (Jonah 3).

The church fasted before sending out Barnabas and Saul, later known as Paul, as missionaries (Acts 13).

The church fasted when appointing elders and committing them to the Lord (Acts 14).

Or fasts that seemed to end in "failure"?

David fasted for his sick infant son. The baby ultimately died, but the fast still served the purpose of drawing David closer to God after a season of rebellion (2 Samuel 12).

What about people who just didn't eat for a few days?

Jonah was in the belly of the huge fish for three days (Jonah 1), and Hannah wept so much about her infertility that she wouldn't eat (1 Samuel 1). I'll let you contemplate those mysteries.

What about Jesus himself?

Jesus fasted for forty days before being tempted in the desert by Satan (Matthew 4).

What about God telling people to fast?

In Joel, the Lord tells the people to return to him with all their hearts with fasting, weeping, and mourning (Joel 2).

In Isaiah, the Lord addresses the heart of fasting (Isaiah 58).

In Matthew 6, Jesus gives instructions for how we should fast.

Check out that line-up. It's a pretty extensive endorsement for fasting, no? Fasting is a vital part of our prayer lives. In fact, my guess is, if you've heard someone preach on fasting, they've referenced that the Bible says "*when* you fast," not "*if* you fast." Those words are directly from Jesus, recorded in Matthew 6:16-18: "And when you fast, do not look gloomy like the hypocrites, for they disfigure their faces that their fasting may be seen by others. Truly, I say to you, they have received their reward. But when you fast, anoint your head and wash your face, that your fasting may not be seen by others but by your Father who is in secret. And your Father who sees in secret will reward you."

The hypocrites made a big show of what they were doing, but even so, they didn't ruin fasting for the rest of us. Jesus still gave us the command despite the possibility we may make a misstep. That's consistent with all of Jesus' teachings—he doesn't let the possibility of failure force us to abandon truth.

Somehow, though, I still let that fear stop me. Have you ever decided not to fast because you didn't want to appear legalistic or do it wrong somehow? Were you ever *planning* to fast, but then you would have had to tell a friend you couldn't meet for lunch and it just felt easier to rationalize that the answer was not to fast at all?

This command is for you and me, and we have to know that before we even dive in. Growing our prayer lives includes fasting. Not *if* but *when*.

I could write a whole book on the reasons to fast, but I want to share just a few that we see in Scripture:

- Nearness to God
- Repentance

- Humbling
- Guidance/direction
- Protection
- Mourning
- Strength in times of temptation

My guess is that you've desired nearness with God, direction, protection, or strength. Or maybe you've needed humbling or space to mourn. Fasting might hold a key to spiritual breakthrough in an area of your life that won't seem to budge. That feels almost too practical for something so spiritual, but God's Word is abundantly clear that fasting plays an important, and often long-lost, role in our faith.

The Blackberry

I was so excited to do it. Fast, that is. Several years ago, my husband started researching the theory that extended fasting could get rid of cancer cells, and that reinvigorated my curiosity about spiritual fasting. Not long afterward, I had been feeling particularly distant from the Lord and decided it was time to stop reading about it and start doing it.

After a morning walk, feeling fresher than I had in a long time, I began making breakfast for the girls—a fruit salad of bananas, apples, strawberries, and Cuties. Then I remembered the blackberries. Oh, I wished I had forgotten we had blackberries. As we all chatted in the kitchen, I mindlessly ate one.

"Oh no! I just ate a blackberry!"

The way I reacted, you would have thought I'd eaten one of those freshness packets they have in new purses. I was bummed mentally, but I could move on. I knew my heart, and this wasn't a defiant statement to the Lord only thirty minutes into my fast. It was an accident. But then my husband responded.

"Oh? Well, you can try tomorrow," he said.

Come again? What was that? Try tomorrow?

I'd felt led to fast on this day and had mustered every bit of energy I had to do it. I was supposed to scrap it because of an accidental blackberry?

Tyler's response rocketed me into an orbit of emotions. I'm someone who has struggled with legalism and who values following the rules, and this sank my previous enthusiasm and readiness to take on the world, making me feel smaller than that errant blackberry.

A series of misunderstood words flowed as he headed out the door, and we continued on the phone trying to get the other person to understand our side. I am ashamed to say I *may have* (okay, definitely) hung up on Tyler when he said, "It's fine! You can pretend to fast today!"

Pretend to fast?

I shrank even more, this time from a full-blown ripe blackberry to a tiny early berry still on the vine. I did not get it. How could I go without a scrap of food from seven thirty in the morning (the time of my ill-chosen blackberry) until the next morning and have it be pretending?

Eventually, Tyler explained his point in words I could hear clearly (you know, without me filtering them through an angst-filled heart), and I got what he was trying to say. Part of fasting involves discipline and a deeper awareness of the Lord. Even though I hadn't scarfed down a burger in willful disobedience, my mindless bite revealed that I wasn't experiencing the awareness a fast requires. Truthfully, I wasn't as alert as I should have been thirty minutes into a day-long fast, so although I wasn't eating, I also wasn't experiencing the fullness of fasting.

Tyler wasn't saying God was angry with me or I'd let him down, but as a perfectionist, that's what I heard. "I've failed God" was how I translated "I wasn't experiencing all God has for us when he calls us to fast."

I'm glad I didn't forget we had blackberries that morning. My mistake opened my eyes to a fuller experience of fasting that I hadn't had before. And this is where I've learned the most about fasting: by actually fasting.

A day of fasting is a day spent fighting my own desires and trading them in for something better. I wouldn't surrender something I love as much as chocolate if I didn't trust that what God offers us is better. When you withhold that bite or resist the urge to lick your finger after serving your kids something with peanut butter, you're telling God he's worth it. You're telling him the long-term goodness that comes from obeying the command to fast is greater than how satisfying that food would taste on your tongue.

Some people can skip meals without skipping a beat. I am not one of them. In mere hours of not eating and seeing the remaining food-less day unfold before me, I want to crumble. And during a recent fast, my own crumbliness revealed just how much I typically cling to my comforts. As I sat trying to resist the prompt to fast that day, I pictured the rich young man we read about in Mark 10. When he asked Jesus how to inherit eternal life, Jesus asked him to sell what he had and give to the poor—and then come follow Jesus.

I pictured myself standing in the rich young man's place,

and Jesus was asking me to close the refrigerator and follow him. I pictured myself saying no and getting to keep my food—but then going away sad, because that's what happened when the rich young man said no. That's what happens when *we* say no to something better too. Of course we're going to go away sad, but somehow we think it's worth it.

When you find yourself saying yes to a day of fasting, finally resisting every excuse you could think of, I want you to remember this: Your sacrifice isn't just a symbolic act. You are telling God with your whole being that you trust his plan more than your own.

Sure, you could *say* that to God. You could journal it and even tell your friends. But have you ever experienced love on paper and then love in action? Love that's backed up with action carries far more weight. I'm learning to love God with an occasionally empty belly, and it's oddly satisfying.

Fruit of a Bloom

A few months after the berry incident, as I found myself staring at a bag of grapes during a fast, it all made sense. It was like scales fell off my eyes. My previous fasts had been all about avoiding something I'd promised God I wouldn't touch. To obey, I had to distract myself in mindless ways because I love food, and the idea of not eating it is way more painful than it should be.

Of course I spent a little more time than usual praying, but I also had many moments of straight-up avoidance. But as I stared at the grapes that day, I was fully aware of my choice to fast. I had decided to take a day to fast and pray for the opportunity to share the gospel with an acquaintance, and as I prayed, my mind was so sharp—no longer fixated on food.

Fasting is not about the void left behind when we take away food. It's about what we put our thoughts on. I could fast on two different days doing exactly the same things, but *how I thought* about it would radically change *how I experienced* it.

Being in the kitchen praying for a lost soul, methodically choosing not to consume even one grape, felt like all my senses were working toward the same goal: to glorify and connect with the Lord. The fast gave me space to think. I wish every day included such slowness and contemplation.

Later on this same day, the bane of my existence threatened to topple me again: a single berry, this time blue. Serenbe, Georgia, where we were spending the month, has blueberry bushes on every corner, and the berries were conveniently ready for harvesting the weeks we were there. Vivi asked to pick a few, and since Tyler was in the neighborhood store getting bug spray, I joined her. A minute later, I realized I'd eaten one. I could not believe it. *Another berry.* I mean, yes, blueberries are good, but trust me when I tell you I can resist a blueberry one thousand times more than I can resist Blue Bell ice cream.

I didn't beat myself up this time, and Tyler was especially supportive. There was something about the hiking adventure we were headed out on that day that had brought me out of my fasting state mentally and into one of pure summertime childlike joy. But I reset and moved on.

Hours later, as I tore Vana's chewy seed-filled bread for her, the sponginess of bread I couldn't eat reminded me to pray. How weird is that? I can't say that I've ever before been led to pray for someone's salvation by the feel of bread in my hands. And if I can paint the full picture, we weren't sitting in our kitchen but on some rocks by a waterfall. I was next to food and away from my phone, fully engaged in the activity at hand—lunch—without the ability to eat. The circumstances sort of forced my hand. Hand on the bread, that is, and I didn't bite. I prayed instead. Each "swift, hard renunciation" as Elisabeth Elliot calls it, is "followed by the sudden loosing of the bonds of self."[1] In other words, every no to self becomes easier—or, at the very least, we become stronger.

It was a beautiful moment in fasting. I was choosing God over things I so often place on his rightful throne. I was finding joy in his ways instead of demanding my own. I could see so clearly the fruit it was creating in me, kind of like those epic examples of fasting in the Bible. But I'm confident that not every fast has yielded such fruit. I promise you some other biblical fasts were of a more mundane variety. How many times had Moses fasted before that mic-drop Ten Commandments–writing mountaintop experience? How many times had Daniel fasted before he amazed kings with his interpretations of their dreams? How many times have people fasted with no miraculous healings or great insight falling from heaven?

Soon after researching fasting, I recalled a season when we fasted as a church each Wednesday. I loved the idea of it becoming a regular part of my prayer life, so each Wednesday morning, I'd spend part of my quiet time asking God what I should pray about during my fast that day and then would spend sunup to dinnertime abstaining from food. As I've been fasting more regularly, I've been reminded firsthand that not every fast brings a miracle of answered prayer or surprising clarity.

One hour before I broke my fast one day, I stood in the kitchen helping prepare dinner and reflecting on the day, acknowledging that nothing magical had happened. I smiled, though. I smiled knowing I'd be doing it again next week. And the next. And the one after that. This is the beauty of repetition at work when it comes to fasting. Our prayers are compounded.

Don't stop praying and fasting because the vine appears to be bearing no fruit. It takes time, and guess what? Continued fasting is a physical way we tell God, *I'm in this. I'm not going anywhere. I believe what you said in your Word, and I will continue to have faith in you, knowing that what I see isn't all there is.* Continuing when you don't see anything happening implies that you believe there is more.

I felt such joy knowing that a seemingly "ineffective" day of fasting didn't mean I was quitting. My faith in the command I've read throughout Scripture wasn't shaken. I wasn't suddenly searching for the meaning of life. *What does this all mean? Is God real? Does he love me? Has he forgotten me?* No. I knew what I knew to be true. And receiving no carrots for my efforts wasn't going to shake that. I truly believe when we keep going without a clear-cut incentive for our prayers, we show God just how much faith we have in him. Not faith in the fact that we'll get a reward. That's easy. *I do this. You do this. I keep coming back.* Dogs are smart enough to do that. But I have faith in the fact that even if I don't get the immediate reward, I'll keep coming back because that's what he's told me to do, and I trust that it is for a purpose.

A Necessary Ingredient

This simple act of denying ourselves in fasting requires an ingredient that is hard to come by in the twenty-first century: humility by way of sacrifice.

It's unsexy in our world of passion and hustle and following your dreams.

It's unflashy in our world that longs for achievements and praise.

It's unseen in our world that measures progress by what is visible.

But fasting is a quick way to *choose* humility as well as to feel humility *happen* to us. We initiate our fast by *choosing* to make a sacrifice, choosing to deplete our own resources in the knowledge that someone else's resources are better. Then, as we move through our time of fasting, we face what we knew would come when we initiated the fast: our complete and utter dependence on the Lord. We experience another layer of humbling *happening* to us as we realize we're empty and need something outside ourselves to fill us.

If you've ever struggled with pride or felt the onset of it and wanted to seek humility, try fasting. I've found it to be one of the quickest ways to strip me of my pride.

Old and New Reminders

I love the Old Testament story of Jehoshaphat, king of Judah, fasting.

> Some people came and told Jehoshaphat, "A vast army is coming against you from Edom, from the other side of the Dead Sea. It is already in Hazezon

Tamar" (that is, En Gedi). *Alarmed, Jehoshaphat resolved to inquire of the* Lord, *and he proclaimed a fast for all Judah.* The people of Judah came together to seek help from the Lord; indeed, they came from every town in Judah to seek him.

2 CHRONICLES 20:2-4, NIV, EMPHASIS ADDED

The next several verses contain Jehoshaphat's long, heartfelt prayer. In verse 12, he prays, "Our God, will you not judge them? For we have no power to face this vast army that is attacking us. We do not know what to do, but our eyes are on you."

When I read this story, I'm struck by how quickly Jehoshaphat decided to fast. He must have been overwhelmed by fear, but that fear was *not* followed by panic, the fetal position, or throwing together a hasty plan that *might* work. He didn't try all other avenues, leaving prayer and fasting as a last resort. He didn't call on the experts in the army or make a stand on the battlefield only to be slaughtered. He released all pride when he leapt into the arms of the Lord. I think our culture would see him as not man enough to handle his own problems. But that's just it—fasting reminds us that we can't handle life ourselves.

Fasting reminds us that we can't handle life ourselves.

And Jehoshaphat didn't merely say, "We can't do this alone, God." He put his money (or his empty fork) where his mouth was and *showed* God through his fasting that he knew who did the saving.

In the New Testament book of Matthew, we see the

disciples attempt to heal a demon-possessed man. And even though they had cast out demons in the past, this time they couldn't. They asked Jesus why, and he told them, "Because of your unbelief; for assuredly, I say to you, if you have faith as a mustard seed, you will say to this mountain, 'Move from here to there,' and it will move; and nothing will be impossible for you. However, this kind does not go out except by prayer and fasting" (Matthew 17:20-21, NKJV).

Pastor David Guzik said, "Little faith can accomplish great things; but great faith can accomplish even greater things. What matters most is what our faith is in, the *object* of our faith."[2] What was the object of the disciples' faith if not Jesus?

I can't help but think that maybe, just maybe, the idea of freeing this man from a demon in front of a multitude led the disciples to dangerously prideful thoughts. Their pride could have been lessened by fasting because of its stark reminder that it was the Lord's power, not their own, that healed. The disciples had healed before (see Luke 9:1-6), and I wonder whether, in this moment, they forgot whose power made that happen. Maybe they thought this time they could do it without faith in God.

The idea that by fasting they could have performed this miracle should prick our ears. I'm not saying we just need to perform a little fast and we'll be blasting out demons left and right, but I wonder what we would be capable of if we lived in this humble state, remembering that the object of our faith is always the Lord. What could happen, not just in our circumstances but in our souls?

Now that we have a little foundation on fasting, let's talk about how we actually incorporate it into our prayer lives.

A Practical Guide to Fasting

1. Don't overcomplicate it.

When I blog about fasting, inevitably a million questions start pouring in about how it works. You might be thinking of a few practical questions yourself. Maybe you take a certain medication that has to be taken with food, or you're pregnant and don't think it's a good idea not to eat.

Let me gently say, don't *look* for an excuse to not fast. You might have a really, really good one, but don't look for one if it's not there. And if you do have a physical reason, choose to fast from something besides food. I'm a fan of fasting from food because that's what we see in the Bible, but even within the broader category of food there are several options. You can skip your favorite meal of the day, fast from a particular food group instead of from all food, or fast from solid food and just drink green juices.

> As you consider what to fast from, I think the biggest question to ask yourself is "Is this actually a sacrifice?"

As you consider what to fast from, I think the biggest question to ask yourself is "Is this actually a sacrifice?" Giving up broccoli, for the 99 percent of us who don't consider broccoli our favorite food, is likely not a sacrifice. It shouldn't take too long to identify what would be a sacrifice for you. A delay speaks to our own hesitation to surrender it, and it might point to just how much we need to give it up.

2. Fast to learn about the power of fasting.

It's nice to do a little research, but I promise, the number-one way you will understand the power and importance of fasting is by actually doing it. My sweetest takeaways about fasting and much of what I shared in this chapter came to me as I experienced it firsthand. So make the commitment right now. You don't need to start fasting this very minute; it's good to prepare your heart and pray about this. But pick a date or time and commit to it.

Reading other stories of fasting can be so encouraging as you fast. I'd encourage you to start with stories of people who fasted in the Bible (see examples on pages 217–218).

3. Have a spiritual goal in mind.

Ronnie Floyd, in his book *The Power of Prayer and Fasting*, says, "Fasting is abstinence from food *with a spiritual goal in mind.*"[3] When you commit to a fast, decide what its specific purpose will be. Repeatedly we see biblical figures fasting for a stated purpose, such as praying for deliverance, direction, or forgiveness. What breakthrough do we hope would come if we fast with nothing in particular in mind?

Are you seeking wisdom, a spiritual breakthrough, or a time of confession and repentance? Journal the specifics, and keep coming back to your goal throughout your time of fasting. Having a purpose in mind will keep you expectant as you trace God's hand at work through the fast.

4. Change the pace of your soul.

We don't always have the option to fast on a slower day, so I'm emphasizing a slower pace of our souls. Even when we're busy, we can take time to be in the moment, remembering that God is present.

Even with my weekly fasts, I haven't had a berry incident since that day on vacation. Not even a lick of peanut butter. It's not because I'm a drill sergeant or suddenly perfect; it's because fasting has slowed down my mind. I've learned to be aware of what I'm doing, and that's created a slower pace in me.

5. Spend extra time in prayer.

Part of the blessing of skipping a meal is being able to use the extra time with the Lord in prayer. Fasting days truly are special because, if you're like most people living in this day and age, finding an extra hour to pray can feel impossible. When you fast, the time is carved out for you already since you'd normally make space for a meal.

6. Spend time in prayer before you break your fast.

Though it sounds so simple, spending thirty minutes with the Lord before you break your fast can give you a chance to praise and thank God for the time you had together and reflect on the day before rushing to the next thing.[4] I've loved spending a little time in prayer, even if surrounded by kids, and I've noticed it slows me down to that first bite. I'm not ravenous or impatient as I finish fasting. Being meditative and slow is a perfect way to break a fast.

Pairing prayer and fasting makes me think of when I was a kid playing video games. In Super Mario Brothers, I'd get a mushroom and, in an instant, it made Mario get bigger and more powerful than he was on his own. He was supercharged. Fasting feels like a supercharging aspect to our prayers that so often we miss out on.

When we throw off the weight of comforts and embrace the discipline of fasting, our prayer lives will be revitalized, and we'll experience spiritual breakthrough.

reflect

Have you fasted before? If not, what has been the weight holding you back? It could be inexperience, fear of giving up something you love, logistics, or something else.

Where are you looking for spiritual breakthrough in your life?

What would it look like on a practical level for you to commit to regular fasting?

read

- ○ Isaiah 58:1-14
- ○ Luke 2:37
- ○ James 1:3
- ○ Matthew 5:6
- ○ Galatians 5:16

15

But for How Long?

Keeping On When I'm Weary

CAN I CONFESS SOMETHING? As I've talked to others about prayer on my blog over the years, I've spent a lot of time making it more palatable. I've tried to emphasize how it can fit into our busy lives. I've talked about prayer on the go. I've comforted the busy mom with toddlers who has trouble spending more than two consecutive minutes talking to God. And while I truly believe God is so gracious to us as we make the most of our time in any season, I feel guilty for neglecting to mention how much sacrifice is involved in prayer. I forgot to mention that we'll find lots of places along the way that tempt us to quit—our doubts, the "nos," our busy schedules, even ministry—and we'll have to persevere.

Leonard Ravenill said, "We cannot have big results from our small praying. The law of prayer is the law of harvest: sow sparingly in prayer, reap sparingly; sow bountifully in prayer, reap bountifully. The trouble is we are trying to get from our efforts what we never put into them."[1] We cannot expect to have the miracles of George Mueller, the thoughtful prayers of E. M. Bounds, or the creative comparisons of C. S. Lewis by giving God the bare minimum.

I feel funny sharing this because I know some will instantly feel guilt or shame, and that's not my desire. My hope, though, is to paint a realistic picture of a prayer warrior. I think our idealistic expectations are ultimately why we feel that prayer "isn't working" or that we're not good at it. Spending ten minutes in prayer every once in a while was never expected to produce a vibrant faith. That's not to say ten minutes of prayer is a waste. It just means we shouldn't come with faulty expectations and then, when they're not met, use them as the excuse to quit that we were looking for.

This is the weight of the journey.

We miss out on the fruit of thriving prayer lives when we give up before things get really good.

If we were sitting together, I'd look in your eyes and express to you how important it is that you keep praying and do not give up. I know you know that, but so much in our world wants to keep us from persevering in prayer. We need the reminders.

It's hard to fully put into words why we should pray. I've come up with about sixty thousand, but I still feel like I've barely scratched the surface. The bottom line is that what happens when I'm in deep continuous communion with the Lord is a slice of heaven. And the world cannot even contain it all. This relationship is the most rewarding we could ever experience.

What would it look like to run hard after God? What

would it look like to sail through roadblocks and distractions without letting them sideline us?

As I imagine it, I see the fullness of joy. I see a peace that passes all understanding. I see hope in eternity. I see victory. I see breakthrough. I see miracles. I see opportunities to intercede for others. I see my soul being restored by still waters. I see wisdom that leads to straight paths.

This can become reality. We can become prayer warriors. We aren't destined for a boring faith that looks like it's gone untouched since 1994. Our God is alive, and so often we forget that because we haven't made a genuine effort to see what he's doing.

We can experience lives that are full of God's presence, responses, and miracles. We can be part of his Kingdom work and be the ones who constantly point people to him. But we need to put in the time.

A year from now, will we be able to say we spent more time with God than we did in the previous year? Or will we make excuses that busy schedules, young kids, a new job, or a world-wide pandemic kept us from praying as much as we hoped?

In his book *The Hour That Changes the World*, Dick Eastman writes, "One hour [of prayer] each day for an entire year equals 365 hours or 45 continuous 'eight-hour' days. Imagine asking your employer for six weeks off work next year so you can spend the time with Jesus praying for the world."[2] When Eastman puts it in these terms, I get so excited for the potential impact more prayer in my life would have. Maybe it's not an hour each day, but maybe it's thirty minutes plus additional little moments through the day. We can do this!

We're always going to have a valid reason not to pray. Martha had good reasons to not sit at Jesus' feet. She was hosting a house full of people. Girl was busy. (See Luke 10:38-42.) But those reasons still were not enough for the Lord. Why? Because God knows what gives us life, and he knows the value of that Netflix show or celebrity gossip we just chose over prayer. Jesus calls us, as he called Martha, to choose what is best—to sit with him and listen to his words.

What's your excuse?

Don't hear me say that like a bully who's throwing you against the locker, adding "chump" to the end of the question. I need to wrestle with this too. What are my excuses for not praying? What holds us back from praying? Like Martha, do we expect the reasons to justify why we can't just sit at the feet of the Lord for a few minutes?

Do we want a life of excuses? Or do we want more of God?

Do we want a life of excuses? Or do we want more of God?

An intimate prayer life will remain a mirage until we admit the changes we need to make as we pursue Jesus.

Encouraging Pray-ers

I could write a whole chapter on encouraging pray-ers, but I'll leave you with three quick stories that may help you visualize what a life of prayer might look like when it's not held back by so many weights.

David. We've talked about David a lot already because the Bible features so many of his actual prayers. Here are a few lessons I've learned from David:

- He pled his case before God (Psalm 25:19-20).
- He comprehended God's timing even when it was hard (Psalm 69:13).

- He knew it was important to share God's faithfulness with others (Psalm 40:10).
- He knew how much he needed God (Psalm 63:1).
- He prayed for wisdom (Psalm 25:4-5).
- He took time to praise God (Psalm 63:5-8).
- He came to God in repentance when he made huge mistakes (Psalm 51).

David was just so . . . human. As I read his psalms, I'm grateful to see what honest prayer looks like. No putting on a show for God. If you can't find the words, David's prayers are a great place to start.

The apostle James. James the brother of Jesus, who is considered the author of the book of James, is apparently referred to as "Old Camel Knees" because he prayed so much. When I heard R. C. Sproul share this fact, the image made prayer so tangible for me. What does a life of prayer look like? Ruddy, old, tired knees? A worn journal covered in prayer requests? A Bible with margins full of dates tracking how God spoke?

The intangibility of prayer can make it hard to figure out. But "camel knees" will forever remind me that prayer requires real things of me, like time and sacrifice. A deep, life-transforming prayer life doesn't happen in drive-by moments. It happens when I keep coming back to the same worn spot. A guitar player's finger calluses develop from frequent playing. If I pick up my guitar one day and then wait two weeks to play it again, calluses

> A deep, life-transforming prayer life doesn't happen in drive-by moments. It happens when I keep coming back to the same worn spot.

don't develop. And camel knees don't result from "Help me!" prayers offered only in hard seasons. They come when we invest serious time and effort.

The thing about calluses is that they make it easier to continue the work we're doing. A guitarist who plays daily doesn't have to nurse painful wounds because her fingers are already toughened up. And a pray-er who comes to God daily isn't constantly trying to remember how to focus or what to say. Her focus muscles and perseverance have prepared her for a consistent relationship.

I want to be the person who doesn't "grow weary of doing good" (Galatians 6:9). Who prays "at all times" and who "keep[s] alert with all perseverance" (Ephesians 6:18). Who has such a sweet rhythm of prayer that calluses develop— not so I grow callous to prayer but so I grow callous to the world's attempts to draw me away. Like James, we can grow in strength and endurance when we practice prayer regularly.

Evelyn Christenson. You've seen her name come up multiple times in this book as the author of *What Happens When Women Pray* and several other books. She was a pastor's wife who began a prayer group with two friends that was originally supposed to last six months. Decades later, after she'd led hundreds of prayer meetings and teaching seminars, she wrote about her experiences, and her books are a "who's who" of Christian leaders from the 1980s. She rubbed elbows with leaders of Promise Keepers, Campus Crusade for Christ (now known as Cru), and more. As I read, though, I got the sense that she didn't fall into this crowd. She was on her knees in prayer as these ministries grew. She wasn't trying to be a part of something big. In one case, she was just praying for a boy from their church (as she and her prayer group did for all the kids from their church), and he later became the assistant to the founder of Campus Crusade for Christ. She was an incredible intercessor, and many of the people she prayed for went on to do big things for God.

Friend, I want to do that. I want God to say, "I'll prompt Valerie because I know she'll pray." I want to have names pop in my head that I can lift up to the Lord, not knowing why I'm called to pray but honored to get to do it even from the comfort of my own bed in the middle of a sleepless night.

Evelyn's life of prayer inspires me to get in this game. I want us to stop sitting on the sidelines offering up prayers for a nourishing lunch or safe travels when we could be interceding for God's work. What can we be doing for the Kingdom that requires only space to hear from God?

Evelyn did some pretty amazing things in her life, but they all hinged on what happened in prayer behind closed doors. Through prayer, we can be involved in Kingdom work that we'd never be able to do in person. We might have no expertise at building schools, but we can pray for those who are expanding education in remote places. We might have no experience changing laws or healing diseases, but through prayer, we can be actively involved in work God is doing to bring justice and show mercy through medicine. The reach we can experience through prayer is incredible.

When You're Weary

As we finish this final weight chapter, I want to encourage you to take action. Decide right now what you want to change about your prayer life. I pray it refreshes you when you feel weary and encourages you to keep pressing forward on the journey of prayer ahead.

1. Grab a friend to take the journey with you.

Having a friend who's chasing after the same goals makes it easier to stay committed. It's why the fittest people are often surrounded by other fit people. Our habits rub off on one another. Imagine doing life with a few friends who constantly ask what they could lift up in prayer for you— friends who, when the hard conversations or the tears come, react first by praying. We're going to have hard moments when we want to give up. I've had those seasons where praying felt almost impossible, and I coveted the prayers of others over me that I could echo. Do this with someone. Don't feel awkward asking. You might just be the answered prayer they've been waiting for. (The Val Marie Paper community is a great supplementary resource online, but we highly recommend going on this journey with someone in your everyday life.)

2. Figure out your heaviest weights.

Throughout this book we've looked at weight after weight that can keep us from running free in prayer. As you read through the chapters, which weight resonated the most? Which ones felt the hardest to shake? Share them with your prayer friends, and ask the Lord to help you remove those weights. Then take the practical steps forward that we mentioned in the book.

3. Study the prayer life of Jesus.

The Gospels are filled with beautiful examples of Jesus escaping from the world to pray. He threw off the weights that could have easily entangled him, and often he chose quiet

Benefits of praying consistently

1. *More focused prayer time.* The more we discipline our minds to pray, the more focus and depth we will experience in our prayers.

2. *A bigger passion for prayer.* The more we experience focused prayer over time, the deeper our passion for prayer will get because we'll begin to see what's possible.

3. *Less anxiety and more faith.* When our eyes are fixed on Jesus and our minds are stayed on God, we find perfect peace (Isaiah 26:3).

4. *A deeper joy.* Even in the mundane moments, when we are in the presence of the Lord, we get to experience the fullness of joy (Psalm 16:11).

5. *Recognizing answered prayers.* When we're praying consistently, we will see God answer prayers. Looking back on these (even when God answers in ways we didn't expect) inspires us to keep praying with confidence.

6. *Living at the center of God's will.* Through praying consistently, we'll hear more from God and will be better able to align our actions with what we hear. And when we're praying over a particular situation, like a job or a move, and receive direction from him, we will have hearts that are willing to obey.

7. *Deeper friendships with others.* As prayer becomes a bigger part of our lives, it naturally becomes a bigger part of our conversations and relationships too. And friendships that are based on prayer are often deep and rich.

8. *Being a part of God's Kingdom work.* The more time we spend in prayer, the more we are available for God to use us for purposes bigger than ourselves, such as people's hearts being turned toward God, justice and peace spreading in the world, and acts of mercy.

9. *Knowing God.* There are thousands of things we won't know this side of heaven, but through a deeper prayer life, we can learn about God and experience him. Knowing him is what we were created to do and where we'll find the greatest fulfillment.

moments with God over the spotlight or sleep. Learn from his teaching on prayer too, as we talked about in chapter 2, reading it in context of everything he taught.

4. Keep learning.

I love that you're reading this book right now, and I encourage you to read other books on prayer. If the topic is on our minds, there's a better chance we'll remember to do it. More knowledge about prayer will also build your confidence. If you've still got lots of questions, talk with a trusted friend or pastor.

5. Make prayer visible.

Prayer is always available to us, but it's also invisible, meaning that we can easily forget about it. This is why goal experts encourage people to make their goals visible. When you can physically be reminded of your goals—perhaps by listing them on a paper taped to your refrigerator or on your desk—you will naturally think of your goals more often. One way to make prayer visible is to write down your prayers in a prayer journal and record your answers. I love our prayer journals at valmariepaper.com, but really, just get something that works for you and will remind you to pray. You could also use an index card with prayers on it as a bookmark, or tape a prayer to your bathroom mirror.

---

tip ——————————————————————————————

Look for ministries or missionaries to support in prayer. Most will be happy to send periodic email updates. Praying for a ministry will naturally increase our hearts for it and help us care more for the work of God's Kingdom.

---

6. Remember the benefits of consistent prayer.

The benefits are extravagant. In the breakout box on page 243 I've shared several that can remind you in those moments when it feels like you're just talking to the ceiling. So much is happening behind the scenes that we cannot see! Prayer is so worth it, and this list can keep you encouraged.

7. Make an actual commitment.

I love this quote that's often attributed to Karen Lamb: "A year from now, you will wish you had started today." Commit today. Write out a prayer, and tell the Lord what you are committing to. Is it a regular practice of fasting? Is it more confession? Is it a specific amount of prayer or a new prayer routine at a certain time each day? Invite God in as you commit to growing in your most important conversation.

———————

What happens next in your prayer story? For too long, I've felt like I was destined for the same song but second verse of prayer failure. What changes all that is knowing that the things weighing us down in prayer don't have to be permanent. And the Lord is ready and willing to work through us. Are we ready to throw off every hindrance? When we throw off the weight of the journey and avoid giving up too soon, we experience the fruit of a thriving prayer life.

reflect

What do you want to change in your prayer life? What are your excuses for not praying?

What are your heaviest weights?

As you make a stronger commitment to prayer, who could go through this journey with you?

read

○ Jeremiah 29:12-13
○ Psalm 27:4
○ Romans 12:12

○ Luke 18:1
○ Revelation 3:20

Epilogue

THIS CHRISTMAS, MY MOTHER-IN-LAW gave me one of the best gifts I've ever received: a first-edition copy of *How to Pray* by R. A. Torrey (1900) that belonged to her mom. The condition was amazing for a 120-year-old book, and the cover boasted a simple serif font and a deep blue-green that might as well have been cherry-picked for this design snob. It's the type of book you hold as if you're holding a newborn baby, careful not to spook it. But here's the thing: As beautiful as the cover is, how sad would it be to display the book on a shelf and never read it when the words inside could be life-changing?

Our prayer lives can be much the same. We can talk about prayer and learn about prayer—but it's the act of praying itself that will be life-changing. We need to enter into our most important conversation remembering this: Of course we'll be imperfect. God never promised we'd master prayer in a day. In fact, he never really said we were supposed to master it in the first place.

But he invites us to talk with him. He wants us to come to him unencumbered by the distractions and insecurities that threaten to steal an intimacy with the Creator that the world will never know. When we say yes to God, it's deep and glorious, and unexpected things happen that can happen only in the presence of the Lord.

We're in the middle of so much turmoil as a country. It's mid-January 2021. You're up to speed on all that's been happening. So many things want to steal our joy and peace.

> **When we say yes to God, it's deep and glorious, and unexpected things happen that can happen only in the presence of the Lord.**

So many things want to convince us God's not real. But as plain as day, when we say yes to more time spent in God's presence, we see that everything we've read about him in Scripture is true. This isn't just for me to experience because I've been talking about prayer for years. This is for every believer who's ready to start ditching the weights.

As you've read the pages of this book, I hope it's been overwhelmingly clear that you are not alone in your struggles to pray. You're not alone in your doubt. You're not alone in your desire to "get it right." You're not alone in your utter insecurity. And you're not the person who dozed off in class when all the prayer warriors learned how to pray.

Whoever told you that prayer should be easy (cough, the devil) lied. It was an attempt to make you feel like a failure so you'd give up before you could get a taste of what awaited you in a thriving prayer life. Prayer isn't easy, but here's the good news: The things that are holding us back, the things that so easily entangle us—we can throw them off. Say it with me. *We can throw them off.*

Fear is not an appendage. Misguided belief is not an

appendage. Our phones are not an appendage. We get to end this book with so much hope because we can change our prayer lives. We'll have to dig in and not be scared of messing it up, but I promise it's worth it!

When I finally cracked open my new favorite deep-blue-green book, Torrey said it better than I could: "Time spent in prayer is not wasted, but time invested at big interest."[1]

When you run this race of a prayerful life, some days may feel like a waste. Some days you'll stumble and fall and wonder what the point is. But when you hop back up, fix your eyes on Jesus. Be reminded that he doesn't ask us to do frivolous things. Prayer is not busywork to get us through life on earth. We're making investments in eternity. We're deepening our relationship with the Lord. We're becoming a part of his Kingdom work. We're learning what it means to live in his presence and respond with obedience. We're growing in faith and hope and becoming more like Jesus. We're entering into conversation with the God of the universe.

And we are not doing this alone. Our God, who's calling us to throw off the hindrances, "is able, through his mighty power at work within us, to accomplish infinitely more than we might ask or think" (Ephesians 3:20, NLT). Oh the possibilities when we involve God! As we pursue lives of prayer, let's run with perseverance—free, unencumbered, and with our eyes always fixed on Jesus.

Prayers to Help Us Throw Off the Weights

IF YOU'RE STUCK on one of the fifteen weights we've talked about throughout the book, try using one of these written prayers to get you started talking to God about how to throw it off.

THE WEIGHT OF EXPECTATIONS

Father God, I want to know you, the real you. Wipe away the expectations I have that don't line up with truth. As I read Scripture, give me an understanding of who you are and how that affects the way I pray. Let me never call into question your behavior before looking into my own. I'm pretty sure I'll discover the answer there. What a privilege to be known and seen by you. Give me a passion to seek you first. In Jesus' name, amen.

THE WEIGHT OF PERFECTIONISM

Father, thank you for allowing us to come to you and for extending so much grace as we do. I feel paralyzed by fear of messing up. Help me to truly see how patient you are with my often messy words and my insecurity that I will do this wrong. I pray that you'd help me come with a heart that is humble, one that comes early and often to a place of confession. Search my heart to see if there's anything offensive in me, and increase my faith. I desperately long to draw near to you and am ready to throw off anything that hinders me. In Jesus' name, amen.

THE WEIGHT OF HESITATION

Father God, prayer can be so scary, not because you are scary but because we aren't really sure we're praying for the right things. I pray, Lord, that you'll fill me with your wisdom. Show me the confidence I can have in coming to you in prayer. Reveal your promises to me and give me an understanding of what they mean for my life. Let me not just bring wishes and dreams that leave me unsure of whether you'll respond. Though I can't predict the future, I can stand on what you've said in your Word and can let that create a firm foundation for me to walk on. In Jesus' name, amen.

THE WEIGHT OF EXCEPTIONS

Father, surrender is hard. Surrender feels like I'm giving up, but remind me, Father, that what I get in return is you. And you are more precious than silver and more lovely than any of your created things. I trust that you love me and you are good, so I give everything to you. Prick my heart when I hold on to things I need to give up. And give me the courage to release them to you so I can pray unencumbered. In Jesus' name, amen.

THE WEIGHT OF EMOTIONS

Father, give me a heart that has no will of its own. Make my

desires your desires, God. I long to tune my heart so closely
to you right now that, as I get up, I can confidently say, "I
will walk in obedience." I know that won't always be easy, but
I pray you would alert me to the beauty of obedience when
my emotions try to lead me any other direction besides pursuing your will for my life. In Jesus' name, amen.

THE WEIGHT OF FACADES

Father, thank you for what a good God you are. I pray that,
no matter what I am experiencing, I would know that. May
I not be afraid to cry to you and let you into my pain. I pray
that I would not stop short with misty eyes but that I would
cry cleansing tears or wails that free up more space in my
heart for you. Heal my hurts and fill me with your truth.
And let me never believe the lie that what I have is too small
or too big to bring to you. In Jesus' name, amen.

THE WEIGHT OF CONTROL

Father, you're never late. Help me to remember that. Your
timing is perfect, while my sight is limited. Help me to fully
trust in your will and your plan. Give me a desire for your
purposes instead of the fleshly desires that keep my prayers
shallow and focused on myself. This conversation is powerful,
yet I settle for so much less when I don't pursue agreement
with you. I am yours and long to glorify you. In Jesus' name,
amen.

THE WEIGHT OF DISTANCE

Lord, I wait for you. It's not easy, but I know it's worth
it. Show me how to respond as I feel overwhelmingly distant from you. Give me patience, Father. I know I am not

forgotten because of what your Word tells me, but help me to believe it with everything in me so that it keeps me coming back to you in this season. Thank you for working behind the scenes right now even when I cannot see it. In Jesus' name, amen.

THE WEIGHT OF EASE

Father, I thank you for this season. Give me words to celebrate you. Let me not get so comfortable or cocky that I venture out on my own without you. Draw near to me. I'm excited to experience this mountaintop in your presence instead of being convinced I can handle it without you. Give me eyes to see whom I can bless. What a true joy it is to sit with you, Lord, in every season. In Jesus' name, amen.

THE WEIGHT OF COMPARTMENTALIZING

Father, you're the God of the universe, and so often I try to tuck you in the proper places of my day and only remember the things about you that make me comfortable. I'm your child, and I want to be a part of your Kingdom work. I want to pray bigger prayers. I want to see you work beyond my four walls. Use me, Lord. And give me eyes to see you through the mundane moments. Help me to take captive any thoughts that don't line up with truth. May I enjoy life in your presence. In Jesus' name, amen.

THE WEIGHT OF SIDESHOWS

Lord, thank you for providing all I need for the spiritual warfare I face. I am not alone. This is your battle. Let me not try to take over, chart the next move, or try to muster up my own strength. Give me eyes to see the real battle and to love others instead of confusing them with my enemy. Protect my mind. Lord, I know so often the victory happens in prayer. So keep drawing me into conversation with you, even if it's the middle of the night. And when you do, may I pop up like Samuel and say, "Here I am!" In Jesus' name, amen.

THE WEIGHT OF SELF-SUFFICIENCY

Father, I need you. I get distracted by the smallest things. And it's not for lack of love; it's just really hard to stay focused. But I'm done letting that be an excuse. Show me how to connect with you in meaningful ways. Help me be intentional about my time with you. Help me find tools that will nurture my ability to focus and enjoy a vibrant conversation with you. You are so worth not leaving my prayer life to serendipity. In Jesus' name, amen.

THE WEIGHT OF MONOLOGUING

Father, thank you for being so willing to speak to me. Forgive me for doing so much of the talking, and teach me how to pause and listen for you. Help me to embrace the awkward silence, and make me expectant to hear from you. I want to treasure your words and ponder the significance of such things. Give me wisdom, Lord, to discern your voice, and give me the courage to obey. In Jesus' name, amen.

THE WEIGHT OF COMFORTS

Lord, I'm yours. I love my comforts, but I love you more. I want more of you in my life, and I want to experience the spiritual breakthroughs that are only possible through fasting. Show me what's possible when I sacrifice the things I love for your glory. Help me step out in faith knowing you satisfy me with your love. You are my great sustainer. In Jesus' name, amen.

THE WEIGHT OF THE JOURNEY

Father, would you carry me on this journey? There are so many spots where I find myself wanting to quit, but in the deepest parts of me, I know that's not a sign to quit. When doubts, distractions, and the everyday give me excuses to stall out, may it be an immediate reminder to keep praying and to push through the obstacles. Your Word is so clear. You are calling me to keep praying and not give up. Show me what that looks like daily, Lord. In Jesus' name, amen.

Acknowledgments

As I STARTED TO WRITE out thank-yous, I quickly noticed a thread. Each person has contributed so much to me and this book. That might sound obvious. Isn't that what this is—a chance to acknowledge who helped make this happen? I may have temporarily forgotten the significance of that. And now I sit here, completely humbled to share a list of people who may occupy just a few typed lines but have done far more than I can pen to a page. How humbling to see how the Lord has rallied troops around me as I share the message of my life.

Tyler. Your support for me and this book gave me confidence (and time!) to articulate the most important message I can share with the world. You deserve far more than a paragraph of gratitude, but you're just so darn humble, I'm not sure you'd accept any more. I'm incredibly honored to get to do life with you.

Alexis, Hannah, Laurel, Mattie, and Natalie. Thank you for stepping out of your comfort zones and saying "yes" when I wanted to start a prayer group. Our time together is never enough.

Kara, Brandi, and Jane. Goodness. Where would this book or VMP be without you ladies? You each were an answer to my prayers as I prayed about the team we would form. It's truly a blessing to see how we all fit and work together for God's kingdom. What a privilege it is to work alongside y'all to motivate people in prayer.

Our Val Marie Paper audience. This book is for you and this book is because of you. Thank you for sharing your questions. Thank you for sharing your insight. Thank you for your support and your prayers. You are changing the world through prayer and action, and I'm just so honored to support you in that.

Sarah, Kara, Karin, Julie, Christina, Kristen, the whole Tyndale team, and Claudia, my agent. We talked a lot about how this would be my legacy book, and I feel you all treated it like it was your legacy book too! Thank you for handling it with such care and always championing me and this book.

Father, what an extraordinary honor it is that you called me to the message of prayer. I'm grateful to call it part of my job to talk about prayer for hours each day. Thank you for using me. I pray you are glorified through this book.

Notes

INTRODUCTION
1. "Infographic: How Is Your Prayer Life?" Crossway, November 2, 2019, https://www.crossway.org/articles/infographic-how-is-your-prayer-life/.
2. "Infographic: How Is Your Prayer Life?"
3. Doug Renner, "It's Time for You to Lay Aside Every Unnecessary Weight," RENNER, accessed January 6, 2021, https://renner.org/article/its-time -for-you-to-lay-aside-every-unnecessary-weight/.
4. *The Biggest Loser*, season 7, episode 17, "Week 17," directed by Neil DeGroot, aired April 28, 2009, on NBC.
5. Darren Hardy, *The Compound Effect* (New York: Vanguard Press, 2010), 105–106.
6. Stephen Nielsen, "Six Weights in the Christian Race — from Hebrews 12:1," *Studying Bible Prophecy* (blog), March 6, 2016, https:// studyingbibleprophecy.wordpress.com/2016/03/06/six-weights-in-the -christian-run-from-hebrews-121/.

CHAPTER 1: WHERE'S MY GENIE IN A BOTTLE?
1. Edward Mote, "My Hope Is Built on Nothing Less," 1834, Hymnary.org, accessed February 16, 2021, https://hymnary.org/text/my_hope_is_built _on_nothing_less.
2. Tiny Theologians created the flashcards. They have the greatest resources for teaching our kids about theology! "Big Words of the Bible," https:// www.tinytheologians.shop/products/big-words-of-the-bible?_pos=2& _sid=41dcf6a79&_ss=r.

CHAPTER 2: AM I DOING THIS RIGHT?
1. Wikipedia, s.v. "Humility," last modified January 31, 2021, 19:17, https:// en.wikipedia.org/wiki/Humility.
2. George Mueller, *Answers to Prayer: From George Mueller's Narratives*, compiled by A. E. C. Brooks (Chicago: Moody Press, 2007), 11.

3. Blue Letter Bible, s.v. "ṣāʿaq," accessed February 18, 2021, https://www.blueletterbible.org/lang/lexicon/lexicon.cfm?Strongs=H6817&t=NASB20.

4. Andrew Murray, *Humility: The Beauty of Holiness* (New York: Anson D. F. Randolph & Co., 1895), 14–15.

5. Murray, *Humility*, 49.

6. Blue Letter Bible, s.v. "rāʾâ," accessed February 18, 2021, https://www.blueletterbible.org/lang/lexicon/lexicon.cfm?Strongs=H7200&t=KJV.

7. Evelyn Christenson, *What Happens When Women Pray* (Minnetonka, MN: Evelyn Christenson Ministries, 2008), 28.

8. Ronnie Floyd, *The Power of Prayer and Fasting: God's Gateway to Spiritual Breakthroughs*, revised and expanded edition (Nashville: Broadman & Holman, 2010), 32.

CHAPTER 3: WILL I EVER GET IT?

1. E. M. Bounds, *Purpose in Prayer* (New York: Fleming H. Revell Company, 1920), 133.

2. David Guzik, "1 John 5 — Born of God and Believing in the Son of God," *Enduring Word Bible Commentary*, 2018, https://enduringword.com/bible-commentary/1-john-5/.

3. Larry Richards, *Every Prayer and Petition in the Bible* (Nashville: Thomas Nelson, 1998), 97.

CHAPTER 4: YOU WANT IT ALL?

1. Michael Weaver and Phil Wickham, lyricists, "Overwhelmed," Word Music, 2011.

2. Natalie Met Lewis, *Wholeheartedly Devoted* (independently published, 2015), 127.

3. *Oxford English and Spanish Dictionary*, s.v. "navel-gazing (*n.*)," accessed December 3, 2020, https://www.lexico.com/en/definition/navel-gazing.

4. Judson W. Van De Venter, "I Surrender All," 1896, Hymnary.org, accessed February 21, 2021, https://hymnary.org/text/all_to_jesus_i_surrender.

CHAPTER 5: WHAT IF I DON'T FEEL LIKE IT?

1. Tim Mackie, "When Pharaoh's Heart Grew Harder," BibleProject, January 21, 2017, https://bibleproject.com/blog/pharaohs-heart-grew-harder/.

2. George Mueller, as quoted in David Guzik, "Study Guide for Genesis 32," Blue Letter Bible, accessed February 21, 2021, https://www.blueletterbible.org/Comm/guzik_david/StudyGuide2017-Gen/Gen-32.cfm.

3. Evelyn Christenson, *What Happens When Women Pray* (Minnetonka, MN: Evelyn Christenson Ministries, 2008), 15.

CHAPTER 6: YOU LOVED THAT WHINER DAVID?

1. Jenn Johnson, vocalist, "Goodness of God," by Jenn Johnson, Ed Cash, Jason Ingram, Ben Fielding, and Brian Johnson, track 3 on Bethel Music, *Peace*, Bethel Music, 2020.

CHAPTER 7: HOW ABOUT WE GO WITH MY PLAN?

1. R. C. Sproul, "Does Prayer Change God's Mind?" Ligonier Ministries, May 1, 2020, https://www.ligonier.org/blog/does-prayer-change-gods-mind/.
2. Lisa T., "Why Are There Four Gospels?" *Beauty Set Apart* (blog), January 15, 2018, https://beautysetapartblog.wordpress.com/2018/01/15/why-are-there-four-gospels/.
3. Tim Keller (@timkellernyc), "God will either give us what we ask for in prayer or give us what we would have asked for if we knew everything he knows," Twitter, November 10, 2014, 2:31 p.m., https://twitter.com/timkellernyc/status/531906966550228993?lang=en.

CHAPTER 8: WHERE DID YOU GO, GOD?

1. Tim Keller, *Counterfeit Gods* (New York: Penguin Books, 2009), xviii.
2. Dick Eastman, *The Hour That Changes the World* (Grand Rapids, MI: Chosen Books, 2002), 37.
3. Horatio Gates Spafford, "It Is Well with My Soul," 1873, accessed February 22, 2021, https://hymnary.org/hymn/CYBER/3106.

CHAPTER 10: CAN YOU FIT IN THIS BOX?

1. Dick Eastman, *Love on Its Knees* (Bloomington, MN: Chosen Books, 1989), beginning of chapter 1.
2. Rick Reed, "How Did Jesus Avoid Temptation?" Daily Commercial website, November 5, 2016, https://www.dailycommercial.com/news/20161105/reed-how-did-jesus-avoid-temptation.
3. Paul David Tripp, *Awe* (Wheaton, IL: Crossway, 2015), 69, 100.
4. A. W. Tozer, *Worship* (Chicago: Moody Press, 2017), 68.
5. John Onwuchekwa, *Prayer: How Praying Together Shapes the Church* (Wheaton, IL: Crossway, 2018), 18.
6. Warren Wiersbe, *Bible Exposition Commentary*, Vol. 2 (Colorado Springs: David C. Cook, 2003), 189.

CHAPTER 11: AM I FIGHTING THE RIGHT THINGS?

1. William Cowper, "Exhortation to Prayer," 1779, accessed February 22, 2021, https://hymnary.org/text/what_various_hindrances_we_meet.
2. Rick Renner, "Spiritual Warfare Is Real!" Renner, accessed November 9, 2020, https://renner.org/article/spiritual-warfare-is-real/.
3. Evelyn Christianson, *What Happens When Women Pray*, 92–93.

CHAPTER 12: CAN I GET A LITTLE HELP?

1. E. M. Bounds, *Purpose in Prayer* (New York: Fleming H. Revell Company, 1920), 47.
2. "Matt Maher - Lord, I Need You (Official Lyric Video)" mattmahermusic, May 1, 2013, video, 3:23, https://www.youtube.com/watch?v=LuvfMDhTyMA.

3. "March 1: Prayer Warriors throughout History—George Whitfield [*sic*]," Prayer Encouragement Project, February 29, 2020, https://2019pray.org /tag/george-whitfield/.

CHAPTER 13: DID YOU WANT TO SAY SOMETHING?
1. John Eldredge, *Get Your Life Back* (Nashville: Nelson Books, 2020), 43.
2. *Oxford English and Spanish Dictionary*, s.v. "expectant (*adj.*)," accessed February 22, 2021, https://www.lexico.com/en/definition/expectant.
3. Max Lucado, *A Gentle Thunder* (Nashville: Thomas Nelson, 1995), 2.
4. Charles Stanley, *How to Listen to God* (Nashville: Thomas Nelson, 1985), 26-42.

CHAPTER 14: ARE YOU SURE THAT COMMAND WAS FOR ME?
1. Elisabeth Elliot, *Discipline: The Glad Surrender* (Grand Rapids, MI: Fleming H. Revell, 2006), 146.
2. Charles Spurgeon, as quoted in David Guzik, "Study Guide for Matthew 17," Blue Letter Bible, accessed December 15, 2020, https://www .blueletterbible.org/Comm/guzik_david/StudyGuide2017-Mat/Mat-17 .cfm, emphasis in original.
3. Ronnie Floyd, *The Power of Prayer and Fasting*, revised and expanded edition (Nashville: B&H Publishing Group, 2010), 128, emphasis in original.
4. I adapted Ronnie Floyd's suggestions from *The Power of Prayer and Fasting*, 131.

CHAPTER 15: BUT FOR HOW LONG?
1. Leonard Ravenhill, *Why Revival Tarries* (Minneapolis: Bethany House, 1987), 119.
2. Dick Eastman, *The Hour That Changes the World* (Grand Rapids, MI: Chosen Books, 2004), 26.

EPILOGUE
1. R. A. Torrey, *How to Pray* (Chicago: The Bible Institute Colportage Association, 1900), 20.

About the Author

Valerie Woerner is an author and the owner of Val Marie Paper, where her mission is to create practical tools and content that equip women to cut through the noise of everyday life and find fullness in the presence of the Lord.

Before starting Val Marie Paper in 2012, Valerie owned a wedding planning business and fell in love with paper design while creating wedding invitations for clients. During her first pregnancy, she created a prayer journal that she desperately needed—and she quickly found that many other women needed it too!

She graduated from Louisiana Tech University in 2007 with a degree in journalism and English. She thought she was destined to work for a big magazine in New York City but found she enjoyed personal column writing more. Her experience designing newspaper pages and her love for writing have come full circle, as she uses both to create content and products that encourage women to transform their lives through prayer and action.

Valerie lives in Lafayette, Louisiana, with her husband, Tyler, and their two daughters, Vivi and Vana. She loves reading, going on barefoot walks around her neighborhood, taking Sunday naps on her screened-in porch, and eating good Cajun food.

To read the blog, shop, or get encouragement from her prayer community, visit the Val Marie Paper website.

valmariepaper.com

Prayer in a Noisy World

@valmariepaper

VMP Society

VAL MARIE PAPER

where prayer meets practical

PROMPTED PRAYER JOURNALS TO:
- ORGANIZE YOUR THOUGHTS
- ELIMINATE DISTRACTIONS
- DEEPEN YOUR FAITH

VALMARIEPAPER.COM

CP1449

WANT A PRACTICAL WAY TO
START PRAYING CONFIDENTLY
AND CONSISTENTLY?

*Grab a prompted prayer journal
from Val Marie Paper.*

DIVE DEEPER WITH THE ONLINE COURSE

Developing a Fluency in Prayer

Immerse in the Culture | The Basics of Prayer

Respect the Culture | The Logistics of Prayer

Embrace Different Dialects | Prayer Techniques

Learn Listening Comprehension | Hearing God

Use the Phrasebook | Prayer and The Word

Address Language Barriers | Breaking Through Obstacles

Practice Conversational Speaking | Praying WITH Others

Become a Translator | Praying FOR Others

Become Fluent | The Benefits of Consistent Prayer

Grab a group and do it together!

VALMARIEPAPER.COM

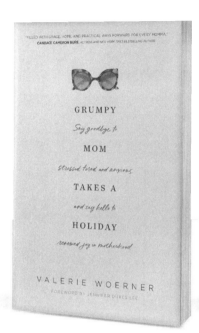

Grumpy Mom Takes a Holiday is the tool you need to help you uncover God's glorious plan for motherhood, complete with satisfaction, rest, freedom from guilt, and an abundance of joy.

Perfect for you or to give to a friend, *Fresh Start for Moms*, a 31-day devotional, will help you stay on track as you become the mom God calls you to be.